GW00643058

LUXURY TRAVEL

COACH DESIGNS IN BRITAIN, 1958–1973

Stewart J. Brown

Capital Transport

First published 1998

ISBN 185414 206 2

Published by Capital Transport Publishing
38 Long Elmes Harrow Weald Middlesex

Designed by Tim Demuth

Printed by CS Graphics Singapore

© Capital Transport Publishing

Top Leyland's Comet was primarily intended for operation as a goods vehicle, but small numbers were sold for use as coaches at the start of the 1950s. Plaxton bodywork is fitted to this example in the fleet of Mandale of Penrith. The Comet was powered by a vertical Leyland 5.08-litre engine. *Photobus*

Centre Most ECW coach bodies on Bristol L-series chassis had concealed radiators, but a small number were built with exposed radiators, including a batch supplied to Eastern National in 1950. Two LL6Bs are seen in 1964 in the ownership of Shephardson of Barton-on-Humber, still in their original owner's livery. *Geoff Lumb*

Right Among the many exuberant designs produced for early underfloor-engined chassis was this style from Willowbrook, seen on two Royal Tigers operated by Black & White Motorways. They were new in 1953. Black & White was a good customer for Willowbrook. At the start of the 1960s 59 of its 98-strong fleet had Willowbrook bodywork. *Geoff Lumb*

Opposite Favourite Service 2 of Bishop Auckland ran six coaches in 1962, all of them Yeates-bodied Bedfords. The two newest, delivered that year, were SB5s with 41-seat Fiesta bodies which perhaps showed Yeates' styling at its most garish. The company's owners were called Harwood, hence the initial H on the body side. *Geoff Lumb*

Title page Most Tilling fleets ran ECW-bodied Bristol coaches. In the late 1950s and for most of the 1960s, the Bristol/ECW combination was synonymous with the express services operated by Royal Blue. Twelve LS6Gs formed the 1957 intake of Royal Blue coaches, one of which is seen at Hastings in 1959, with an older Bristol behind. These coaches were owned by Western National and are seen operating on the South Coast Express to Bournemouth. *Frank Mussett*

Front cover Harrington's Crusader III body on a Thames operated by Garelochhead Coach Services, who bought three of this combination. It was new in 1963 and is seen outside Helensburgh railway station. *Harry Hay*

Back cover Bedford's twin steer VAL was an eye-catching coach. Coliseum of Southampton operated this early example with Duple Vega Major body, inspected by a couple of Southdown drivers in Hastings coach park in the summer of 1963. *D N Warren*

Contents

Introduction

This book on coach design covers the period from 1958 and the opening of Britain's first stretch of motorway, an event which was to lead to dramatic changes in travel patterns, to 1973, when the bulk of the established network of coach routes in England and Wales was about to be rebranded under the National banner.

Today there is a much greater distinction between buses and coaches than at any time in the past. Apart from the Volvo B10M – Britain's best-selling coach – virtually all of the chassis being sold in Britain are used exclusively either for bus or for coach use – not for both. This wasn't the case in the mid-1960s, when the four most popular single-deck chassis – Leyland Leopard, AEC Reliance, Bedford VAM and Ford R-series – were designed to be equally suitable for coach or bus bodies.

Similarly, the bodies being built now tend to be either buses or coaches. In the 1960s it was rather different. True, the main builders – Plaxton and Duple – were building pure coaches. But the three big operating groups had a fondness for dual-purpose vehicles which were suitable for either coach or bus operation depending on the demands of traffic. Thus the Scottish Bus Group used the Alexander Y-type; the BET companies had that organisation's standard 36ft single-deck body with either bus or coach seats; and the state-owned Tilling group operators used Bristol REs with either genuine Eastern Coach Works coach bodies or with coach seats in an ECW bus body shell.

During busy periods in the 1960s, extra journeys on coach services would often be covered by buses. Duplicates on Ribble express services to Blackpool, for example, could be double-deck buses. At the Glasgow Fair holiday, 20-year-old Leyland Tiger half-cabs could be found running alongside new Y-type AEC Reliances on express services to Fife coastal resorts. When large crowds wanted to be moved, coach operators were loath to say no.

Quite what the once-a-year coach traveller thought of going on holiday in a double-deck bus or a 20-year-old half-cab is difficult to imagine. One can only presume that just as the 1990s motoring holidaymaker travelling at peak summer weekends accepts the twin discomforts of endless queues on the motorway and overcrowded service areas, so his (or her) counterpart in the 1960s accepted that their conveyance from home to holiday destination might not be the last word in luxury.

I had some direct involvement with coaching in the mid-1960s, working for Alexander (Midland). This company was Glasgow's main coach tour operator, with an extensive programme of Scottish and English holidays, and of day excursions. On peak summer Saturdays and Sundays up to 100 vehicles would be dispatched on excursions, starting with full-day tours to far-flung destinations such as Oban and Dunoon at 8.30am, and finishing with evening mystery tours departing typically until around 6.30pm. As the day wore on, the search for available vehicles and drivers grew ever more desperate. Coaches arriving in Glasgow on express services would be sent off on excursions, and when

A classic 1960s coach in a classic tour location. The vehicle is a 1963 AEC Reliance with what might be considered the definitive version of Plaxton's early 1960s Panorama body, with its almost straight waistline. Earlier 36ft Panoramas, although broadly similar, had a more pronounced dip in the waist towards the rear, and also had a smaller windscreen. It is seen on tour in the Scottish Highlands in 1966, on the main road between Kinlochleven and Glencoe. A Vauxhall Victor follows. *Iain MacGregor*

A decade of coach design at Doncaster Racecourse in the summer of 1971. On the left is a rare Burlingham Gannet body on a Bedford SB chassis, dating from 1962 and looking distinctly old-fashioned. In the centre, a Leyland Leopard illustrates one of the high-points of mid-1960s styling with its Plaxton Panorama I body. On the right is the latest Plaxton Panorama Elite II, on a Seddon Pennine chassis. *Michael Fowler*

the supply of coaches dried up, buses, including elderly lowbridge PD2 Titans, would be used.

There was a steady flow of work in the summer for part-time weekend drivers who would cover local bus services, releasing full-timers for hires and tours. And it was not unknown for bus drivers to work a double shift on a busy summer Saturday, starting work at 5.30am and finishing at 11pm, all to release more drivers for coach work.

The private hire business was booming too. There were the traditional day trips to the seaside, Sunday School outings and works trips. Teenagers who in the 1990s take their girl-friends out in ageing XR3i Fords with expensive sound systems had to hire coaches in the 1960s. They would appear in the private hire office – always at least three of them – looking for a price for a coach for a Saturday evening trip to Edinburgh, setting off at around 6.30pm, usually from some doubtful street corner in Glasgow's east end. They'd want to leave a minimal deposit, with the balance being paid to the driver before the coach set off.

It was Alexander (Midland) policy to avoid this type of work, and any one of the warning signs mentioned above would provoke either the response that we were fully booked, or would produce a price so high as to be unrealistic. The work was unfair to both the drivers – who had to put up with a coach load of drunks – and to the coach, which wouldn't always survive unscathed. Generally we were able to weed out such bookings, though some got through – including one where an exceedingly respectable youth made the booking on behalf of his mates, bestowing further respectability by giving the start point as a church hall. We didn't fall for that trick twice.

One of the things which sets coach operators apart from bus operators is the way in which they buy vehicles. In 1960 a bus operator would buy a new bus in the expectation that it would provide between 12 and 15 years of service and would then be sold for further use or for scrap. But coach operators had different aims. There's a lot of fashion in the coach business, and most operators buying a new coach in 1960 would expect to run it for no more than five years, at which point they would take it to a dealer and trade it in as part exchange against a new one – a bit like a motorist changing his or her car. The dealer would then sell the old coach, which

could quite commonly have five or six owners in its life.

There was a network of specialist coach deal-ers supplying new and used coaches – a mid 1960s issue of *Commercial Motor* included in its classified columns:

Arlington Motor Co in Potters Bar
(for many years renting part of the London Transport garage)
E J Baker & Co (Dorking)
Birmingham Coach Sales
Comberhill (Durham) Garages
Erringtons of Evington
Don Everall Commercial Vehicles, Wolverhampton
Stanley Hughes & Co, Bradford
Kirkby and Sons (Sales), South Anston
Luton Commercial Motors
Millburn Motors in Glasgow and Preston
(whose adverts for used coaches always included registration numbers, to the delight of enthusiasts)
Alf Moseley in Loughborough,
(who claimed to be Britain's largest PSV distributors)
Nash of Cardiff
Shaw and Kilburn of Acton
SMT Sales and Service Co in Glasgow
("with a national reputation for square deals")
and
W S Yeates in Loughborough.
Most were selling Bedfords and Fords.

The dealer network and the operators' need to trade-in coaches when they wanted to update their fleets militated against the unconventional. Buy a new Bedford or a

W. Alexander & Sons Ltd
Private Hire for Private Parties
Glasgow District

Thames with bodywork by Duple or Plaxton and you could be sure that after a couple of years in service it would command a reasonable trade-in value. The same couldn't be said of coach bodywork from Willowbrook, Weymann or Park Royal for example, which in part explains why these builders never really succeeded in the coach business, no matter how good their products might have been.

This constant process of fleet updating also set the independent coach operators apart from most bus operators running coaches. Big bus fleets would aim to run a coach for the same length of time as a bus, but with gradual demotion from front-line tours and hires to, ultimately, bus and contract services.

In many areas coaching – like bus travel – was in decline throughout the 1960s. The new opportunities which the motorways opened up for coach operators were often cancelled out by the continuing rise in car ownership. Many of the holiday-makers who in 1960 took an express coach to the seaside and then used local operators' excursions to get around had, by 1970, acquired a car or were holidaying in Spain.

So the story in this volume is one of change. It covers a period when the last old-fashioned half-cab coaches disappeared, and new coaches grew bigger, from 30ft to 36ft and then to 12m. The story closes in 1972 when there were new body ranges being launched by Plaxton and Duple. Since then there has been something of a coaching renaissance. The 1980 Transport Act deregulated coach operation and revitalised express services. Throughout the 1980s coaches grew more powerful, air suspension was adopted as standard, and body specifications became ever more luxurious. But that, as they say, is another story.

My thanks to those who have helped in the preparation of this book, including Stephen Barber of Wallace Arnold; Stuart Jones of the weekly trade magazine *Bus & Coach Buyer*; Jim Leach, who worked for Duple during much of the period this volume covers; Geoff Mills; Reg Monkhouse, a Leyland service engineer in the 1960s; Phil Palmer of the West Midlands Vintage Vehicle Society; Roger Phillips, a director of Arlington who retired from the coach business in 1994; Roy Smirk, who over a 40-year career sold coaches for Yeates, Plaxton and Duple; Bob Smith, a former colleague from my days at Leyland; Ian Studd, a long-standing employee of Duple at both Hendon and Blackpool; Philip Thornes of Thornes Motor Services; Bob Vale of Bob Vale Coach Sales, who worked for Arlington from the early 1960s until that company ceased dealing in coaches and who then set up his own successful dealership; George Wedlake – and the many other contacts I have among coach dealers and operators who over the years have added to my understanding of this vibrant industry.

Many photographers produced fascinating material from their collections, and these are individually credited. The photographs credited to Chris Aston and Martin Llewellyn are available from the Omnicolour archive, run by Chris Aston.

Carefree by Coach

'EAST KENT' OPERATE
FREQUENT EXPRESS SERVICES
DAILY BETWEEN
LONDON (Victoria Coach Station)
and the main towns in the **SOUTH-EAST**

★ Coach Holiday Tours.
★ Europabus Coach Services throughout
    Western Europe.
★ Inclusive Day Tours to Canterbury.

Enquiries welcomed at

VICTORIA COACH STATION,
LONDON, S.W.1

or at the address shown on the front cover.

EAST KENT
ROAD CAR COMPANY LTD

STATION ROAD WEST, CANTERBURY. Tel: Canterbury 6615

NOW IN OPERATION

Direct Services to and
from Chelmsford -
Colchester - Clacton -
Northampton - Leicester and Nottingham

I have to say I was pleasantly surprised by
the amount of high-quality colour material
available on coaches, and grateful to those who
generously made rare and valuable original
transparencies available for use in this volume.

A number of people kindly commented on
the draft text, namely John Aldridge, Maurice
Bateman of AVE Berkhof, Gavin Booth, Jef
Johnson, Colin Rowland of Rambler Coaches
and Ray Stenning. But, as always, any mistakes
or erroneous conclusions can be laid at my
door, not theirs.

The 1960s was an interesting and colourful period in coaching. I hope you enjoy
reading this volume as much as I enjoyed
writing it.

Stewart J Brown
Reedley Hallows, 1998

SEE THEM NOW! TRY THEM NOW!

Body by Duple

Body by Harrington

Body by Plaxton

RING **WATerloo 4959** NOW!

also **A.1 USED COACHES**
wide selection available
come and see them *NOW!*

Dispatch Motors

On show at DISPATCH MOTORS—
the Thames 41-seater chassis fitted with
exclusively designed bodies by Duple,
Harrington and Plaxton. They're the
finest coaches on the roads for operating
economy and passenger comfort! Order
the coach of your choice with the well-
tried, smooth-running Thames 6-cyl-
inder engine for petrol or diesel.

FORD DISTRIBUTORS

Arrange for a free demonstration today!

98-120 SOUTHWARK BRIDGE ROAD · LONDON S.E.I · WATerloo 4959

Bus & Coach, April 1960

SHAMROCK & RAMBLER Motor Coaches Ltd

Booking Office & Coach Station
77 Holdenhurst Road,
Bournemouth Phone 27616

BOURNEMOUTH'S LEADING COACH TOUR ORGANISERS

*Daily Tours and Excursions to all Places of
Beauty and Interest in the
South & West*

Branch Offices at Bournemouth Pier, Sea Road, Boscombe and
Fisherman's Walk ★ Agents throughout the district

TRAVEL BY **CHILTERN QUEEN** COACHES

This 1952 Dennis Falcon with
Gurney Nutting bodywork was
bought by Chiltern Queens in 1958. It had
previously been operated by Yellow Bus of
Guildford. By 1964, when this photograph was
taken, it had been relegated to contract work, a
common fate for elderly coaches of obsolete
design. *Geoff Lumb*

The late 1950s: changes ahead

On 12 December 1958 Britain's first stretch of motorway opened. It was the eight-mile-long Preston bypass, relieving a notorious bottleneck on the main A6 road which ran through the town centre and crossed the River Ribble on the only available bridge – the first on the river estuary and one with no real alternative for north-south traffic.

The opening of this short stretch of motorway heralded the beginning of a new era in road transport (and provided Ribble with the opportunity to run excursions along the Preston bypass at 2s a head). It would soon be followed by the first stretches of the M1 in Northamptonshire and within 10 years Britain would have 560 miles of motorway in use, with many more under construction.

But back to 1958. The operators themselves fell into four main groups. In Scotland, the Scottish Omnibuses Group was easily the main provider of coach services. Each of the Scottish group's subsidiaries ran coaches. Generally these were dual-purpose machines, typi-cally with Alexander bodywork on AEC or Leyland chassis. A few Bedfords were opera-ted, with bodies by Duple and Burlingham, and two Scottish Omnibuses Group compa-nies ran Bristol coaches.

In England and Wales both the BET and Tilling groups ran coaches, generally as an adjunct to their bus businesses, although there were some dedicated coach companies in both groups, such as BET's Sheffield United Tours operation, or the Tilling group's London-based Tillings Transport. The BET fleets ran a remarkably wide range of coach types, while the Tilling fleets in the main ran ECW-bodied Bristols. As in the Scottish Omnibuses Group, there was a tendency to favour dual-purpose vehicles which could be used for inter-urban bus services as well as for coach duties.

The three big groups were primarily run-ning buses, but ran coaches too because it seemed like a logical extension of their busi-nesses. Their coach operations ran with vary-ing degrees of success – and with the all-important protection of the system of

Yelloway Motor Services of Rochdale was a highly-respected operator. It ran express services from Blackpool to London which headed south from Manchester through Stockport, Macclesfield, Leek, Derby, Loughborough and Leicester. Two of its first Harrington Cavaliers, on AEC Reliance chassis, are seen in Derby bus station on their way south. They were from a batch of six delivered in 1961. By 1965 there would be 31 Cavaliers in the Yelloway fleet. *Martin Llewellyn*

Right above The majority of coaches operated by the Scottish group were in reality dual-purpose vehicles, usually with bodywork by Alexander. This style of body with its curved waist and short centre bay was supplied on a range of chassis including, unusually, the Bristol MW as seen here in Carlisle. Only Western SMT took this Bristol/Alexander combination. This was a 1958 coach; the last bodies of this style were on seven MWs for Western SMT in 1962. Over a ten year production life there were detail differences between batches of bodies. Not all had a grille on the front and some had flush-mounted side windows. *Paul Caudell*

Right below BET group companies ran a wide variety of coaches, often specifying less luxurious vehicles for express work, such as this Willowbrook-bodied Leopard. The first 36ft-long Willowbrook bodies for BET had flat glass screens, and users included Yorkshire Traction, with three of these Leopards in 1962. They operated as 47-seat coaches until 1969 – the expiry of their initial seven year Certificates of Fitness – when they were rebuilt as 53-seat buses. *Iain MacGregor*

Road Service Licensing which had been set up by the 1930 Road Traffic Act.

Indeed, there has long been a line of thought that bus operators are not very good at running coaches, and it has to be said that it was among the fourth main group, the independents, that coaches without compromise were most often to be found. Unencumbered by the dead hand of big bus company bureaucracy, the independents – generally small family-run businesses with an entrepreneurial bent – concentrated on coaching, with vehicles bodied by the leading builders, Burlingham, Duple, Harrington and Plaxton. Even if in the late 1950s they didn't quite spell it out this way, the independents were in the leisure business. A number ran regular express coach services – operators such as Barton Transport, Grey-Green, Premier Travel and Yelloway – but most were in the private hire business (which was outside the Road Service Licensing net) while many ran day excursions and holiday tours.

Coach operation by municipal fleets was rare. The main exception was Edinburgh City Transport, with its established programme of local tours. At the end of the 1950s these were being run primarily by Leyland-bodied Royal Tigers which had been delivered in 1952 as rear-entrance buses but had been converted to front-entrance coaches – using the word coach in its loosest sense – in ECT's workshops in 1958-59. Other municipal

Below At the start of the 1950s ECW built 20 coach bodies of an attractive style on AEC Regal IV chassis for two operators – London Transport and Tillings Transport. Compared with the over-embellished confections being produced by some coachbuilders at the time, ECW's body was a model of restraint. It was also arguably more attractive and more coach-like than the bus-based coach bodies which followed. Tillings Transport had its Regal IVs rebodied (by ECW) in 1960 and one of the displaced bodies found its way to Taylor of Glasgow, mounted on an ex-Western SMT Regal IV chassis. The Ford Consul grille was added by Taylor. *Iain MacGregor*

Right Advertised excursions were controlled by the strict Road Service Licensing system and at the start of the 1960s were still a worthwhile source of income for many independents. McConnachie of Campbelltown operated this classic Duple-bodied Bedford SB, seen plying for custom on the sea-front. It is offering a Machrihanish tour for two shillings. *Harry Hay*

operators whose fleets included vehicles which might be considered as coaches in the early 1960s were Aberdeen, Bolton, Bournemouth, Chesterfield, Coventry, Leeds, Liverpool, Llandudno, Manchester, Salford, St Helens and Wallasey. Those in Liverpool and Manchester were in reality airport buses, and in some of the other towns the main reason for owning a coach was to provide transport for committees of local councillors. Most municipal transport departments were prevented from operating beyond their own boundaries without special authorisation. This helped dampen whatever little coaching flair may have been hidden among local authority transport managers.

London Transport's coaches also stretched the use of the term. The RTs used on Green Line services differed little from their bus counterparts. LT's private hire fleet comprised AEC Regal IVs – 25 RFs with 35-seat Metro-Cammell bus bodies and 15 RFWs with unusual ECW coach bodies. All 40 had glazed cove panels, invaluable for urban sightseeing, and the RFWs were 8ft wide (hence the RF Wide type code) and boasted high-backed seats. Incidentally, five RFW-style bodies were supplied by ECW to Tillings Travel, also on AEC Regal IV chassis, and ran until 1960 when they were replaced with the latest style of ECW coach bodies.

Coach operation in 1958 was under tight licensing control. Road Service Licences, issued by 11 area traffic commissioners, were needed for express services and for excursions and tours. On express services the licence would fix the route, the timetables and the fares to be charged. The licence would also specify where passengers could be picked up and set down. Any changes had to be agreed in advance. Where the service ran through more than one traffic area – which, by their very nature, most express services did – the operator would need to hold what were known as backing licences to authorise operation through other traffic areas. These were often only a formality, but they still took up management time.

Much the same applied to tours. A day tour licence would specify a starting point and pick-up points, list all of the routes and destinations to which tours could be operated, specify the fares, and possibly place a limit on the maximum number of coaches which could be operated on any one day. For holiday coach tours there was the additional complication of backing licences, and of

Below Cheltenham coach station was an important interchange for express coach services. Identifiable in this late 1950s view are coaches operated by Royal Blue, Western National, Black & White, Southdown, and Red & White. The Black & White coaches are Willowbrook-bodied Royal Tigers, while the Southdown vehicle is a Beadle-bodied Tiger Cub. The other coaches, all owned by Tilling companies, are assorted types of ECW-bodied Bristol. *Frank Mussett*

authorisation for local excursions – known as fantails – from the resort in which the coach holiday was based.

Surprising as it may seem now, fantails were often the subject of controversy. For example, in 1963 Edinburgh Corporation objected to a proposal by Eastern National to run a half-day city sightseeing tour as part of a Scottish holiday tour. Eastern National would be using its own coach, and only carrying its own passengers who had travelled up from England – but still Edinburgh Corporation felt that its existing city tours should be used by Eastern National's customers while they were sightseeing in the Scottish capital.

Applications to vary licences, or to apply for new licences, were often hotly contested by other operators and by British Railways, all anxious to protect their businesses from any perceived threat from a new operator or from a change to an existing operator's established pattern of services. It was even possible for shipping operators to object, as occurred when Rhondda applied for a licence to run from South Wales to Minehead and to Bournemouth via the new Severn bridge. P&A Campbell, which ran seasonal shipping services across the Bristol Channel, was one of the objectors to this proposal.

Licence applications were heard in traffic courts, where the traffic commissioners would hear evidence from the applicant and from the objectors, before reaching a decision on whether or not to grant a new licence or to vary an existing one. It was a cumbersome procedure, and one which favoured the status quo.

This controlled competition saw the formation of what could be described as cartels, where express service operators pooled their

ASSOCIATED MOTORWAYS
REGULAR SERVICES
Day and Night EXPRESS COACH SERVICES

MIDLANDS & SOUTH WALES TO SOUTH COAST & SOUTH WEST

SOUTH WEST TO MIDLANDS & SOUTH WALES

FOR "ROYAL BLUE" EXPRESS COACH SERVICE FACILITIES SEE INSIDE FRONT COVER

ANY ASSOCIATED MOTORWAYS AGENCY OR

ASSOCIATED MOTORWAYS. HEAD OFFICE. COACH STATION, CHELTENHAM SPA. PHONE 3611

Left **Although barely 10 years old, half-cab coaches such as this Dennis Lancet with Duple A-series bodywork were considered distinctly old-fashioned by the late 1950s. The Lancet with its high-set radiator aged less gracefully than some of its competitors. The operator is Horseshoe Coaches of Tottenham.** *Capital Transport*

Lawson's **Land Cruises** from Glasgow

Season 1961

resources to provide, in fairness, a better service to travellers. The best known of these pools was Associated Motorways, which saw seven Tilling operators – Bristol, Crosville, Eastern Counties, Lincolnshire, Red & White, Royal Blue and United Counties – plus Black & White Motorways and BET's Midland Red run a co-ordinated network of services covering much of England with interchange facilities at Cheltenham. Coaches converged on Cheltenham coach station – opened in 1931 – from all points of the compass with the main arrivals of the day being timed to link with a mass departure at 2pm. The 2pm coaches ran to destinations which included London,

Aberystwyth, Bangor, Cleethorpes, Eastbourne, Great Yarmouth, Ilfracombe, Nottingham, Paignton, Pembroke Dock, Swansea and all points in between. Independent Yelloway of Rochdale provided links to the North West. Associated Motorways had been formed in 1934 and would survive until the creation of National Travel in 1973.

Westlinks, set up in 1952, was a link-up between Ribble, Scottish Omnibuses and Western SMT running services from Scotland to destinations in Lancashire with onward connections to South Wales and the South West of England using the Associated

Motorways network. In all such pools the coaches ran in the operators' own liveries, with the pool name being purely a marketing tool to promote the range of co-ordinated services on offer.

In 1958 there were some 20,000 coaches in use in Britain. A few prewar survivors could still be found, generally relegated to rural bus services in quiet backwaters. Early postwar coaches were still around in large numbers. The late 1940s had seen feverish activity among coach manufacturers, catering for the pent-up demand for travel which had been released when World War II ended. In the late 1940s front-engined half-cab

Left **Rebodying was one way of updating obsolete half-cabs. This 1947 Leyland Tiger PS1 was rebodied by Plaxton in 1956 for its original owner, Hunter of Seaton Delaval. It is seen later in its life running for Galley of Westerhope – one of the constituents of the Tyneside PTE's Armstrong-Galley coach operation in 1973.** *Iain MacGregor*

HIRE A COACH FOR YOUR PRIVATE PARTY

Quotations and suggestions for itineraries on enquiry at any of the Company's local offices

Below **A few coachbuilders routinely built fully-fronted bodies on front-engined chassis, most notably Burlingham with the Sunsaloon and, as shown here, ECW. Western National operated this 1951 Bristol LWL6B, seen in Victoria Coach Station in the early 1960s running on a Royal Blue service. Broadly similar coaches were supplied to a number of Tilling group companies.** *Paul Caudell*

Bottom **Dennis was one of a number of manufacturers to fade from the coach business in the 1950s. Its last big coach order came from East Kent, which took 30 Lancet UFs with Duple Ambassador bodies in 1954. The last survived in service until 1971.** *Gerald Mead*

coaches were the norm, typified by models like the AEC Regal III and Leyland Tiger, with bodies by a bewildering variety of small builders cashing in on a buoyant market.

Many of the coaches of this era had bodies by manufacturers who had quickly vanished into obscurity – such as Beccols, Bellhouse-Hartwell, Picktree, Scottish Aviation, Trans-United (which was associated with Yelloway) and Windover, to name but a few. Small builders like these sold their products primarily to local operators. By 1958 most of these first generation postwar coaches had been downgraded to mundane duties such as local private hires and works or school contracts, largely because they had been rendered obsolete almost overnight by the appearance in 1950 of a new generation of underfloor-engined chassis which made the front-engined models with their exposed radiators seem distinctly old-fashioned.

Some bodybuilders addressed this problem by offering full-width cabs on bodies for front-engined chassis, while some operators tried to add a touch of modernity to older coaches by grafting new full-width fronts on to old bodies – W Alexander & Sons, Wallace Arnold Tours and Dodds of Troon were among companies to do this. Such modernisation certainly made pre-1950 coaches look more attractive to travellers, but clearly didn't bring them up to the improved standards of ride and comparative silence of the mid-engined models.

Late buyers of half-cab coaches included Western National with Bristol LLs in 1951 and W Alexander & Sons with OPS2 Tigers in 1952 which were divided between its famous Bluebird fleet and its subsidiary company David Lawson of Kirkintilloch, whose touring holidays were promoted as Lawson's Land Cruises.

A few operators bought new front-engined coaches with fully-fronted bodies. The last front-engined coaches bought by Black & White were Bristol L6Gs with fully-fronted Duple bodies, delivered in 1948. They lasted until the early 1960s. Unusually these retained their exposed radiators – most fully-

Mulliner of Birmingham took a brief interest in the coach market, building two striking coaches in 1959 on Guy Warrior chassis. The project was not a success. One of the coaches is seen in 1965 in the fleet of Rennie of Cairneyhill. The body originally had a sliding entrance door. Note the air horn mounted ahead of the door. *Iain MacGregor*

fronted coach bodies made some effort to conceal the radiator. W Alexander & Sons bought Daimler CVD6s with full-front ECW bodies, of a style more commonly fitted to L-series Bristols for Tilling companies. Burlingham offered its customers the Sunsaloon, with a full-width front. One drawback of bodies of this design was that they impeded access to the engine.

So, in 1958, most front-line coaches in large fleets were mid-engined types. Leyland and AEC were clear leaders in this field, but there were smaller numbers of less common types still to be found – the Guy Arab UF and LUF (favoured by Western SMT for its prestigious Glasgow to London service), the Dennis Lancet IV (used mainly by East Kent which had 30 with centre-entrance Duple bodies), the Daimler Freeline, and low-volume models from Atkinson (which built just 20 coach chassis between 1951 and 1956), Seddon and Sentinel. Seddon produced its last mid-engined coach chassis in 1958 – but would reappear later.

Alongside the Gardner-engined Arab, Guy also produced a lightweight Warrior LUF in small numbers from 1956 to 1961. Launched with a horizontal four-cylinder Meadows engine, Guy tried unsuccessfully to broaden the Warrior's appeal by offering other engines, including the Gardner 5HLW. The most interesting Warriors were two built in 1958 with futuristically-styled Mulliner coach bodies – an eye-catching design which caught the imagination of Triang, who included one in their 1/42 scale Spot-On range of die-cast models. With the Warrior, Guy disappeared from British coaching. One of the Mulliner-bodied Warriors was an exhibit at the 1958 Commercial Motor Show.

The Daimler Freeline had a choice of Gardner or Daimler engines and was never really popular with coach operators, although in an outburst of local loyalty Red House Motor Services of Coventry bought six with Burlingham Seagull bodies. Daimlers were built in Coventry. The biggest UK Freeline coach user was Blue Cars of London, which had eight with Bellhouse-Hartwell bodies. In 1958-59 the Freeline was nearing the end of the road and in these two years only seven Freeline coaches were delivered to British operators – Plaxton-bodied examples to Pyne of Harrogate (one) and Burwell & District (two), one with a Burlingham body to Blue Bus of Willington (a long-standing Daimler user), and three

Below **The Albion Aberdonian was offered by Leyland as a lighter alternative to the established Tiger Cub. A number of coach operators bought Aberdonians, but the biggest user of the model was W Alexander & Sons, which bought 22 in 1957-8. An Alexander (Northern) Aberdonian, with 41-seat Alexander body, arrives in Aberdeen in 1964. The dual-purpose nature of most Scottish Bus** Group coaches allowed vehicles such as this to be used on long bus services – although, with its heavy single-piece in-swing manual door, this style of Aberdonian was unlikely to be popular with conductors. *Harry Hay*

Far right ECW's rather bus-like coach body could offer more comfort than at first appeared. South

Midland took delivery of four Bristol MW6Gs in 1960 which had 34 seats compared with the standard 39 or 41. One is seen in Oxford in 1970, wearing its 10 years lightly. It is on the London to Oxford express service. *Iain MacGregor*

Willowbrook-bodied vehicles to Coventry Corporation. Daimler then disappeared from coaching – for the time being at any rate. It had supplied 69 Freeline coaches to British operators.

The last Foden coach entered service in 1958, a rear-engined chassis with Plaxton body for Toppings of Liverpool. The chassis had in fact been built in 1951 and had been used for testing by Foden. It brought to just over 50 the number of rear-engined Fodens sold to British coach operators.

Beadle of Dartford, who had been active in building new coaches using old running units at the start of the 1950s, had pulled out of coach production in 1957. Its Rochester integral coach, restyled for 1957, had in fact sold fairly well with 78 being delivered including 20 for Southdown; 12 for Smiths of Wigan; eight for Yorkshire Woollen and smaller numbers going to such well-known fleets as Don Everall of Wolverhampton, Timpson, Devon General (whose coaches ran under the Grey Cars name), PMT and Valliant

Direct of Ealing. The Rochester was powered by a horizontal Commer TS3 two-stroke engine of just 3.26-litre capacity and rated at 105bhp.

The original underfloor-engined models from both AEC and Leyland had been heavy. The Regal IV used AEC's 9.6-litre engine in a coach which typically weighed around 8 tons, which was more than most contemporary double-deck buses. Leyland's Royal Tiger was just as heavy, and was powered by that manufacturer's O.600 unit. Both the AEC and Leyland engines were rated at 125bhp.

New, lighter, mid-engined coach models appeared from 1953 – the Reliance from AEC and the Tiger Cub from Leyland. These were over one ton lighter than their predecessors,

and used smaller engines. AEC offered the 6.75-litre AH410 (98bhp) or the 7.7-litre AH470 (112bhp), while Leyland provided the 5.76-litre O.350, rated at 108bhp for coach use. The new models were more fuel-efficient than those which they replaced and, by and large, had enough power to cope with the road conditions of the day when dual-carriageways were very much the exception rather than the rule. The lower-powered Reliance was short-lived.

The lightweight Tiger Cub was joined by the even lighter-weight Albion Aberdonian in 1957. This used the same engine – the Leyland O.350 (Albion had been a Leyland subsidiary since 1951) – but in a chassis with a lighter frame which shaved half a ton off

FOR LUXURY COACH TRAVEL STIPULATE "WESTERN NATIONAL"
CLUB SECRETARIES AND ORGANISERS GIVEN EVERY ASSISTANCE
Address your enquiries to any of the Company's Offices shown on page one.

the unladen weight. Aberdonians found a limited role as coaches – the biggest user was W Alexander & Sons, with 22, all of which were Alexander-bodied. But a few found buyers elsewhere, usually with Plaxton bodywork. Charlie's Cars of Bournemouth ran Aberdonians with Harrington coach bodies. The Aberdonian was built at Albion's Glasgow factory and production ceased in 1960.

Albion did, incidentally, sell small numbers of front-engined FT-series Victors in the late 1950s. Bodybuilders included Duple (with a Vega-style body), Strachan and Yeates who supplied one of the last, in 1960, to Court of Nuneaton.

Bristol, too, was building coach chassis, but purely for sale to the state-owned Tilling and Scottish groups. These were the LS (Light Saloon) and then from 1957 the MW (Medium Weight), powered by either a six-cylinder 100bhp Bristol AVW engine, or by Gardner's 5HLW or 6HLW, five- and six-cylinder units rated at 95 and 112bhp respectively. All of the Bristols built for Tilling companies were bodied by Eastern Coach Works, but in Scotland Western SMT took both LSs and MWs with Alexander bodies to a

Left **Alexander built occasional non-standard coach bodies, such as a batch of 20 on AEC Reliance chassis for Scottish Omnibuses in 1959. These were 38-seaters for use on the tourist services connecting Edinburgh and London, and were generally known as the "two-day Reliances" – that being the length of time one of the services took. They did not have the short bay amidships which was a hallmark of Alexander bodies on mid-engined chassis in the 1950s. The cove panels and front dome were glazed. This one is seen in the Trossachs in 1961.** *Iain MacGregor*

Right **Plaxton's Panorama was the first real threat to Duple's supremacy in the coach business. Sheffield United Tours was the first operator of the Panorama, and quickly standardised on it. The polished horizontal side beading was an SUT feature, but it was also specified by a few other operators.** *Chris Aston*

Right below **An idyllic setting for an AEC Reliance with Duple Britannia body, from Duple's 1961 publicity material. The operator was Samuelson New Transport Co of London.**

SCOTTISH OMNIBUSES · SEASON 1962

London Edinburgh
sightseeing services
Two, Three and Four Day

specification which was more dual-purpose than true coach.

The Construction & Use Regulations limited two-axle coaches to a maximum length of 30ft, and within this most bodybuilders aimed to provide 41 seats. Toilets were unusual, with the main users of toilet-equipped coaches being Western SMT and Scottish Omnibuses, for the 400-mile-long services which each company ran to London from Glasgow and Edinburgh respectively. Western was using centre-entrance Guy Arab UFs; Scottish Omnibuses ran AEC Regal IVs. And even though toilets were fitted, the long journey was still punctuated by stops for rest and refreshment at Lockerbie and either Grantham or Newark.

At the start of the 1960s the Glasgow to London service, for example, took almost 14 hours and required two drivers. (Thirty years later this would be cut by almost half to 7 hours 30 minutes for the fastest timing on National Express.) The day service – summer only – left Glasgow at 7am and was scheduled to arrive in Victoria Coach Station at 10.54pm. The year-round night service was given the same length of time, leaving Glasgow 12 hours later and reaching London at 10.54am. The precision of the timings – which included Gretna (AA Box) at 10.38 and Penrith (Crown Hotel) at 11.43 – had more to do with the vagaries of the Road Service Licensing system, which required precision in running times and speeds, than the realities of long-distance coach operation. Add 11

optional stopping points in Scotland and 15 in England and the word "express" to describe the service seems to be stretching the point. But express it was, and Western's coaches gave a spirited performance as they headed up and down the A1, the route used to get from Scotch Corner to London after a trip down the A74 and across the undulating A66.

Scottish Omnibuses also ran leisurely two- and three-day tourist services between Edinburgh and London, with overnight stops on route. These used 38-seat coaches without toilets – from 1959 a batch of 20 Alexander-bodied Reliances of a unique design.

In 1958 there were five coachbuilders meeting the majority of the body requirements of independent coach operators – Burlingham, Duple, Harrington, Plaxton and Yeates. In addition Roe was selling its Dalesman in small numbers, while Alexander was supplying coach-type bodies to Scottish group companies, and ECW was building for the Tilling group. Bus builders Weymann and Willowbrook were building relatively small numbers of coaches, primarily for BET group companies.

The outstanding DUPLE-A.E.C. BRITANNIA as supplied to Samuelsons New Transport Ltd.

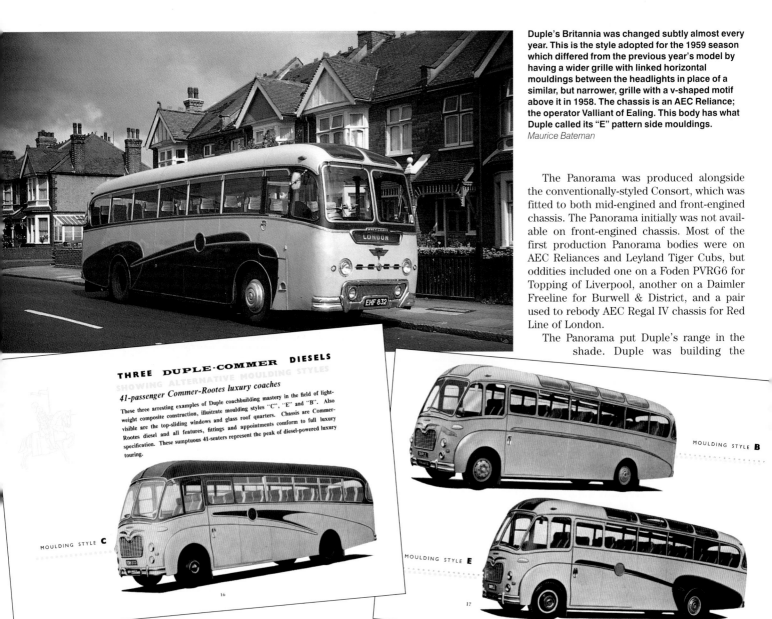

Duple's Britannia was changed subtly almost every year. This is the style adopted for the 1959 season which differed from the previous year's model by having a wider grille with linked horizontal mouldings between the headlights in place of a similar, but narrower, grille with a v-shaped motif above it in 1958. The chassis is an AEC Reliance; the operator Valliant of Ealing. This body has what Duple called its "E" pattern side mouldings.
Maurice Bateman

The Panorama was produced alongside the conventionally-styled Consort, which was fitted to both mid-engined and front-engined chassis. The Panorama initially was not available on front-engined chassis. Most of the first production Panorama bodies were on AEC Reliances and Leyland Tiger Cubs, but oddities included one on a Foden PVRG6 for Topping of Liverpool, another on a Daimler Freeline for Burwell & District, and a pair used to rebody AEC Regal IV chassis for Red Line of London.

The Panorama put Duple's range in the shade. Duple was building the

THREE DUPLE·COMMER DIESELS
SHOWING ALTERNATIVE MOULDING STYLES

41-passenger Commer-Rootes luxury coaches

These three arresting examples of Duple coachbuilding mastery in the field of light-weight composite construction, illustrate moulding styles "C", "E" and "B". Also visible are the top-sliding windows and glass roof quarters. Chassis are Commer-Rootes diesel and all features, fittings and appointments comform to full luxury specification. These sumptuous 41-seaters represent the peak of diesel-powered luxury touring.

MOULDING STYLE **C**

MOULDING STYLE **B**

MOULDING STYLE **E**

A trend-setting coach body was unveiled in 1958, the appropriately-named Panorama from Plaxton. The first, for Sheffield United Tours, was built on an AEC Reliance chassis. The Panorama featured three main side windows, each 6ft 8in long, compared with five windows on the comparable Consort body, from which the Panorama was derived. This reduced the number of main body pillars from seven to four. Concern about the strength of coach structures in roll-over accidents was not a major issue in 1958.

The Panorama, with its straight waist and clean-cut lines, seemed light years away from some of the curvaceous excesses of just eight years earlier with the first generation of underfloor-engined chassis. In 1958 SUT's Panorama won the 4th British Coach Rally, held at Brighton, and a Grand Prix d'honneur at the Nice coach rally, where it was the only British entrant. Early Panorama buyers included Wallace Arnold, Cotter of Glasgow, Gardiner of Spennymoor and Straws of Leicester.

SUT and Plaxton were setting the pace at this time, and at the Geneva show in March 1959 there was an SUT Panorama on display with a simple Smiths air-conditioning system, designed to maintain the interior temperature at 4degF below that outside.

Super Vega and the generally similar Britannia at its Hendon factory. The pretty 41-seat Super Vega with its distinctive butterfly grille was mounted on the Bedford SB chassis; the Britannia was fitted to underfloor-engined models and was available with either a front or centre entrance. Front-entrance Britannias had an inward-opening door (liable to deposit road dirt on the clothes of boarding passengers who brushed against it) while on centre-entrance bodies a sliding door was used. An un-named body, similar to the Super Vega but slightly taller

Above **The most common version of the Duple Donington had small side windows and curved windscreens, as illustrated by a Tiger Cub in the unusual livery of Carruthers of New Abbey. Based on a Leyland Tiger Cub chassis, it had been built as a stock vehicle for Millburn Motors, the Glasgow-based dealer.** *Iain MacGregor*

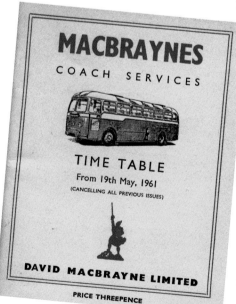

MACBRAYNES

COACH SERVICES

TIME TABLE

From 19th May, 1961

(CANCELLING ALL PREVIOUS ISSUES)

DAVID MACBRAYNE LIMITED

PRICE THREEPENCE

and with a simpler one-piece grille, was offered on the Commer Avenger. The Vega, incidentally, was named after a star.

Duple's coach bodies in the late 1950s were available with different styles of polished mouldings on the sides, known rather prosaically, as B, C and E. These are more easily described by pictures rather than words. Duple did launch a variant on the Super Vega theme for 1958 – the 37-seat Alpine, which was in effect a Super Vega with a Perspex roof and one row of seats removed. But while Plaxton's Panorama went from strength to strength, the Alpine vanished into obscurity – although the name would be revived. One was built for Dickson of Dundee, but carried Vega badging.

One other significant event in coach building in 1958 was the takeover by Duple of Willowbrook. Duple, with a factory in Hendon, was primarily a builder of coaches, although it did build small numbers of utilitarian bus bodies, mainly on Bedford SB chassis. Willowbrook was based in Loughborough and did build coaches, mainly for BET companies, but most of

its output was buses – including small numbers of double-deckers. The two businesses thus complemented each other.

Willowbrook's coach was the Viking and customers included Devon

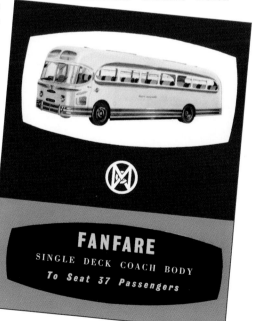

FANFARE

SINGLE DECK COACH BODY

To Seat 37 Passengers

General (16 Reliances for its Grey Cars fleet in 1958-59) and Northern General (10 Reliances in 1959). North Western took five Reliances in 1960 which had Viking bodies with longer windows. The only other big-name user was Coventry Corporation with its three Freelines, and total Viking output was below 40. The Viking was named after the operator of the 1957 prototype, Viking Motors of Burton-on-Trent.

Duple already had a subsidiary in the East Midlands at Kegworth, Duple (Midland), created following the acquisition in 1952 of Nudd Brothers & Lockyer. Duple (Midland) built steel-framed bodies, including the Donington on mid-engined chassis which was the standard MacBrayne coach for a time and was also specified by Lancashire United, Timpson, Sunderland District, Yelloway and a number of smaller businesses including Scout of Preston (who would be bought by Ribble in 1962), Pennine of Gargrave, Carruthers of New Abbey and Hutchison of Overtown. The Duple (Midland) and Willowbrook businesses were gradually merged on Willowbrook's Loughborough site.

Weymann, big in bus building, was on the fringes of coaching. At the 1954 Commercial Motor Show it had launched the Fanfare, with the first being on an AEC Reliance for North Western. Unusually for a coach of this period it had an all-metal body. More followed, though not in large numbers. The Fanfare was bought mainly by BET companies, namely Devon General, Neath & Cardiff, North Western, Northern General, PMT, Rhondda, South Wales Transport, Southdown, Trent, Wakefields and Yorkshire Woollen as well as Timpson, which was owned jointly by BET and Tilling. Between them these fleets accounted for around 120 Fanfares out of a total production of 144. Northern General's were unusual in being built on Guy Arab LUF chassis. The only significant customer outside the BET group was the Sheffield Joint Omnibus Committee, while the only Weymann Fanfares bought by independents were three for Robin Hood of Nottingham (which was taken over by Barton Transport in 1961) and six for Birch Bros – all on AEC Reliance chassis. Salford Corporation bought one Fanfare for use as a committee coach.

Weymann built two batches of coaches for Western Welsh who shunned the Fanfare and instead opted for a unique design with a straight waist, sloping pillars and an unusual four-piece windscreen in which the two centre sections were curved in a style described as arcuate. There were 21 in all and they entered service in 1960 and 1961 and served Western Welsh until 1970. One other Weymann body deserves a mention – the export Arcadian. This was built on a left-hand-drive Leyland Royal Tiger Worldmaster chassis in 1956 and was in effect a stretched high-floor version of the Fanfare, 34ft long and 11ft 9in high with Stone air-conditioning and underfloor lockers. What makes it of interest is that it had three main side windows – two years before Plaxton's Panorama – and anticipated the use of long windows in the final batch of Weymann Castilian coach bodies for Southdown seven years later. The solitary Arcadian was exported to Spain.

Another company whose main business was building bus bodies was Charles H Roe of Leeds, part of the Associated Commercial Vehicles organisation which owned AEC and Park Royal. Roe, like Weymann, dabbled in coach production with its Dalesman body most of which, perhaps not surprisingly, were built on AEC Reliance chassis. The Dalesman was an attractive design which belied its

Left The Weymann Fanfare was a distinctively-styled body, most examples of which were bought by BET companies. These included Neath & Cardiff Luxury Coaches. N&C ran 35 coaches – mainly AECs – and its main operation was an express service from Cardiff to Swansea. Three Fanfares were purchased in 1958. *Chris Aston*

Below Bespoke coach building was becoming increasingly unusual by 1960 when Western Welsh took the first of two batches of Weymann-bodied AEC Reliances. Where other BET fleets which bought Weymann bodies took the Fanfare, Western Welsh had bodies to this design with fewer windows, a straight waist, and sloping pillars. This body style was unique to Western Welsh. Most were 36-seat touring coaches and were christened the Cambrian class by Western Welsh, while similar 39-seaters were called the Celtic class. *Glyn Bowen*

builder's bus-manufacturing background. It was introduced in 1954, and was then updated in 1955, 1956 and in 1959 when Black & White took five of the latest – and last – incarnation, the Dalesman IV. Ten Dalesman IVs were built with the other five going to small operators. Over six years total Dalesman output totalled 68, 24 of which were for one operator, Essex County Coaches, where by 1959 they accounted for the bulk of the 30-strong fleet based in Stratford, East London. Sister ACV company Park Royal built very few coaches in the 1950s but it did supply significant numbers of dual-purpose vehicles to BET companies in the early part of the 1960s, most notably on AEC Reliance chassis to East Kent and Aldershot & District.

One other English bus body builder, Northern Counties, built a batch of coaches – eight bodies on Leyland Tiger Cub chassis for Lancashire United Transport in 1960. Northern Counties was the major supplier of bus bodies to LUT and these were really buses with coach seats, some polished exterior mouldings and glazing on the front dome. Most LUT coaches of this time were somewhat bus-like and the fleet included Duple Doningtons and a small batch of Burlingham coaches which had bus body shells.

Scottish body builder Alexander, which moved from Stirling to a brand new factory in Falkirk in 1958, sold few bodies in England in the 1950s. The company was primarily a bus builder, although some of its coaches were quite luxurious, such as the centre-door Coronation style bodies built on Royal Tigers for W Alexander & Sons and on Guy Arab UFs for Western SMT and Central SMT. In 1953 a new forward-entrance coach body

Although not offered in the UK market, MCW's Arcadian was the first British-built coach with long side windows, anticipating the Plaxton Panorama and also the final version of MCW's own Castilian. Only one Arcadian was built, on a left-hand drive Leyland Worldmaster chassis.

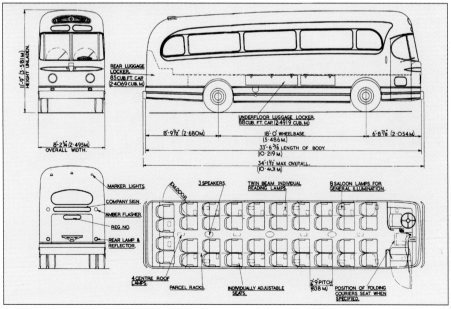

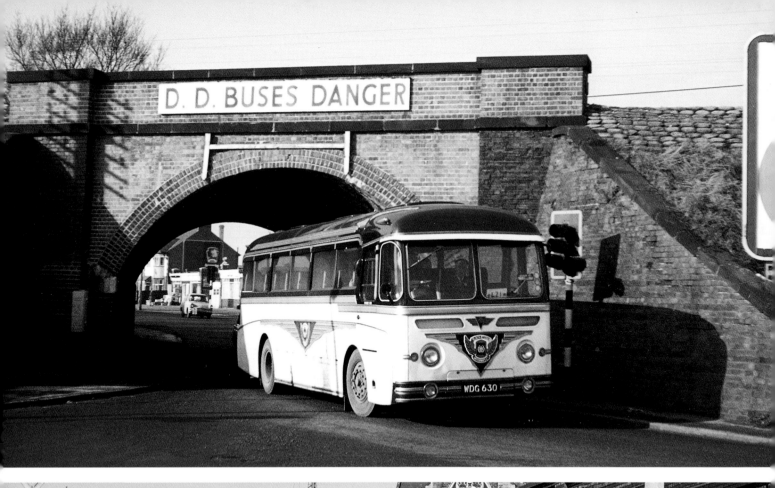

Top left **The final version of the Roe Dalesman had sloping window pillars. Customers included Black & White Motorways. All Roe Dalesman bodies were built on AEC Reliance chassis – Roe and AEC were sister companies within the Associated Commercial Vehicles group.** *Chris Aston*

Bottom left **Barton Transport bought small numbers of Alexander bodies. This one, on a Reliance chassis, was a cramped 43-seater. It was new in 1958. This style of body was usually associated with Scottish group companies which received examples on AEC Reliance, Albion Aberdonian, Bristol LS and MW, Guy Arab LUF and Leyland Tiger Cub chassis. The front mouldings and destination display were to Barton's specifications.** *Iain MacGregor*

was introduced, with a curved waistline – following earlier straight-waist coaches this was in some ways a retrograde step – and gently curved windscreens, a significant innovation at a time when flat glass was still the norm. This body was specified by Leyland for four Tiger Cub demonstrators, which may have helped raise Alexander's profile in the south. It secured low-volume business from a small number of English fleets including Barton Transport (which took 13) and the associated fleets of Smith and Webster in Wigan, taking eight between them.

Alexander had in 1957 introduced a new straight-waisted dual-purpose body which retained the pillar spacing of the 1953 design, including the short bay in the middle which housed the emergency door. This was supplied mainly to

Scottish group companies on Reliance and Tiger Cub chassis, along with a few on Albion's short-lived Aberdonian. There were detail design improvements over the years – it lasted until 1962 – with the most distinctive being a dozen 38-seat coaches supplied to Highland Omnibuses in 1961-62 which had additional side mouldings, glazed cove panels, a single-piece inward-opening entrance door (in place of the standard jack-knife type) and glazing on the front dome.

The same basic structure was used for 20 coach bodies on Leyland Tiger Cub chassis for Alexander (Midland) in 1961, the company formed to take over the southern area operations of W Alexander & Sons and the associated David Lawson business. These had attractively-styled glass fibre front and rear mouldings, with the rear having a reverse-rake window of the style briefly made popular by Ford's use of it in 1959 for its new Anglia saloon. The idea was also used – less subtly – by Willowbrook on its Viscount design. Incidentally, the creation of Alexander (Midland) brought an end to Lawson's Land Cruises and the cream and maroon coaches used on them, but not of Alexander's Bluebird insignia, which survived the changes.

At the start of the 1960s Duple and Harrington bodies tended to dominate in southern fleets, with Plaxton and Burlingham bodies selling more strongly to northern operators. New Harrington bodies, for example, were very rare in Scotland. In London, most of the major fleets were standardised on Hendon-built Duple bodies – a choice which guaranteed good spare parts support. London area fleets which were made up entirely of Duple-bodied coaches bought new included Lewis Cronshaw (19 vehicles), Samuelson New Transport Co (14) and Venture Transport (11). Venture Transport was taken over by Lewis Cronshaw in 1961.

The mighty George Ewer group – owners of such well-known companies as Grey-Green and Orange Luxury – ran 140 coaches of which 108 had Harrington bodies while

the remainder were bodied by Duple. New Plaxtons in the capital were in a minority although Plaxton was starting to make inroads, with operators such as Fountain Coaches of Twickenham taking 10 Embassy bodies on Thames Traders in 1960.

London was, of course, the busiest centre for long-distance coach services. From Victoria Coach Station (opened in 1932) there were direct links to all major towns and cities in England and Wales, and across the

Perhaps the prettiest coaches built by Alexander were 20 Tiger Cubs for Alexander (Midland) in 1961. These still used the standard body shell, but made full use of the potential of glass fibre to produce stylish front and end mouldings. A fire at Alexander's coachworks destroyed the moulds and this batch of coaches remained unique. This shot was taken in Aberdeen. *Harry Hay*

Scottish border to Glasgow and Edinburgh. Through services to destinations north of central Scotland were still in the future. Victoria Coach Station was owned by London Coastal Coaches, controlled jointly by the Tilling and BET groups. London Coastal Coaches also owned the Samuelson coach business.

Despite the intensive network of rail services provided by British Railways Southern Region, there were reasonably frequent coach services from Victoria to points on the south coast. East Kent ran via Canterbury to Margate and Ramsgate with something approaching an hourly frequency. The company also served Deal and Dover. Sister BET subsidiary Maidstone & District served Maidstone, Sheerness, Hastings and Bexhill. Southdown had services to Eastbourne,

Brighton, Worthing, Littlehampton, Bognor, Hayling Island and Southsea. The fastest timing to Brighton was two hours non-stop. BR could do the trip in half the time – but at a much higher fare. The Southdown stopping service between London and Brighton actually took only half-an-hour longer than the non-stop coach; the A23 road offered little scope for fast running.

Other operators in the South East with regular services to Victoria were Aldershot & District from Farnham; Thames Valley from Reading; South Midland from Oxford running either via High Wycombe or Maidenhead and taking 2 hours 45 minutes; United Counties from Nottingham and Northampton; and Eastern National from Southend-on-Sea. Eastern National and Thames Valley used forward-entrance Bristol Lodekkas on their

busiest services, with the former's generally being in an adaptation of the company's Tilling green livery in which cream was the main body colour. Between 1962 and 1968 Eastern National bought 15 FLF Lodekka coaches, primarily for use on the London to Southend service which ran via Southend Airport. They had but 18 seats in the lower deck, with space for luggage at the rear. The service to Southend Airport had started in 1956 when it carried 10,000 people. So successful was it that by 1962, when the first FLFs were introduced, it was carrying 200,000 people a year.

While Victoria was London's flagship coach terminal, it wasn't the only one. In Pentonville Road there was King's Cross coach station, run by PSV Operators and providing services to Essex and East Anglia

which reflected the geographical distribution of those companies which were members of PSV Operators. These included Jennings of Ashen, Norfolk Motor Services of Great Yarmouth, Premier Travel of Cambridge, Suttons Coaches of Clacton-on-Sea, Whippet Coaches of Hilton, Yelloway Motor Services of Rochdale, and a host of London area operators such as Banfield, Battens Coaches, Blue Belle, Lewis Cronshaw, Empire's Best, Fallowfield & Britten, Horseshoe Coaches, Lacey's, Mitcham Belle and Orange Luxury.

Express services were operated from King's Cross by Jennings to Thaxted, Clare and Ashen; Norfolk Motor Services to Colchester, Lowestoft, Great Yarmouth and Hemsby; Premier Travel to Saffron Walden and Haverhill (but not to Cambridge, which was an Eastern Counties service); Suttons to Clacton and Jaywick Sands; Whippet to Biggleswade and Huntingdon; and Yelloway to Manchester, Rochdale, Blackburn and Blackpool. Grey-Green also ran from King's Cross to East Anglia.

Other London terminals included Timpson's in Catford; Orange Luxury in Brixton (running mainly to coastal towns in Suffolk, Essex, Kent, Sussex and Hampshire); Empire's Best, with a daily service from its Peckham coach station to Clacton (via central London, Enfield, Epping and Chelmsford) and Frames Tours with its underground coach station and garage in Herbrand Street.

Eastern National had its own King's Cross coach station (from 1963, in Tillings Transport's Pentonville Road garage) with services to a variety of places to the east of London. Eastern National also had a Wood Green terminal, originally used by the City Coach Co (which had been acquired by Eastern National in 1952) and operated from Wood Green to Southend. This was in reality a long limited-stop bus service, rather than a true coach operation.

Among the features influencing the changing appearance of coaches were advances in technology and changes in legislation. A legislative change in the late 1950s removed the requirement for buses and coaches to have an opening windscreen. This paved the way for the use of the comparatively recent technological advances in glass manufacture which enabled the production of large curved windscreens, a feature which was being used increasingly on cars. Developments in glass fibre, too, would play a big part in shaping coach bodies. Out went complex compound curves which had to be shaped by a panel-beater. In their place came even more complex shapes which could be produced in glass fibre using a mould.

The Plaxton Panorama may have been setting new standards for coach design and the first short stretch of M6 motorway may have been providing a pointer to the future, but there was still a strong conservative ethos among many operators. In May 1958, ready for Scotland's short summer season, drivers working for W Alexander & Sons were given a little booklet containing advice on driving on tours and hires. It advised the driver that "he should be smartly dressed – his uniform should be tidy, the jacket buttoned up properly, and the uniform hat must be worn at all times." It didn't mention the use of white tops on tour drivers' hats, a practice which survived into the 1960s with many large operators.

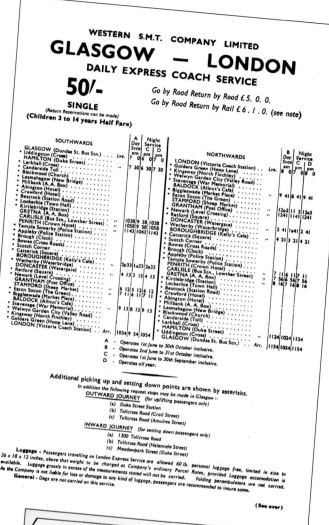

Motorway opportunities

The opening of the embryonic motorway network was to bring new opportunities to coach operators and manufacturers.

Two BET group companies were among the leaders in this field. W C Standerwick of Blackpool, a Ribble subsidiary since 1932, ran services from Lancashire to London. In the late 1950s these were generally entrusted to Leyland Royal Tigers, which headed south to the capital down a network of A roads which included some dual-carriageway bypasses, but were still largely single-carriageway and heavily trafficked. The 230-mile journey from Blackpool to London was scheduled to take no less than 12 hours, with 8am departures from both ends of the route reaching their destinations at 8pm. The solidly-built Royal Tigers gave a firm ride and were reasonably quiet by the standards of the day.

Ribble had some limited experience of running double-deck coaches with its fleet of White Ladies, Leyland Titans with stylish fully-fronted bodies by Burlingham and East Lancs. But the new double-deck coaches which started to enter service with Ribble and Standerwick from 1959 were a far cry from the White Ladies. They were the Gay Hostesses – a name which might provoke a wry smile now, but which was quite innocuous in 1959. For the Gay Hostess, Ribble took Leyland's new rear-engined Atlantean chassis and had it fitted with a Weymann body which was equipped as a coach. A standard bus-bodied Atlantean seated 78 passengers – 44 up and 34 down. The comfortable Gay Hostesses had but 50 reclining seats – 34 in the top deck and 16 in the lower saloon. At the rear of the lower deck there was a toilet compartment, a servery and space for passengers' luggage. There were also overhead racks on both decks, with individual reading lights. The steward or hostess served tea, soft drinks, biscuits, sandwiches, sweets and cigarettes. Externally the box-like appearance of the standard BET group rear-engined double-deck body of the period was considerably improved by the use of polished mouldings. Translucent roof panels gave added light to the interior.

The Atlantean chassis, powered for this application by Leyland's 153bhp 11.1-litre O.680 engine (rather than the standard 125bhp 9.8-litre O.600), had air suspension on the front axle, although this proved troublesome and was replaced by conventional steel springs. By 1961 there were 37 Gay Hostesses in the Ribble and Standerwick fleets. With an unladen weight of 10 tons, the Gay Hostesses were at that time the heaviest psvs ever to have operated in Britain. They gave 10 years service and by using the available sections of the M6 and M1 motorways they had slashed the Blackpool to London running time from 12 hours to as little as 6 hours 39 minutes for the fastest service in the mid-1960s.

Ribble sought permission from the traffic commissioners to use the Gay Hostesses on excursions and tours. It succeeded with its tours licences from Preston, Blackburn and Liverpool, but in Morecambe the local coach operators' association objected on the grounds that it would increase Ribble's capacity to the possible detriment of their own business.

The other pioneering motorway coach came from that most indi-

★ **Gay Hostess**

RIBBLE STANDERWICK

A new style double-deck luxury coach for long distance express services

The Gay Hostesses brought new standards of comfort to Standerwick and Ribble express services from the north-west of England to London. They were Leyland Atlanteans with lavishly-equipped Weymann bodies. The basic boxy shape of the standard bus shell was cleverly disguised by the use of polished mouldings and Standerwick's livery. *Gerald Mead*

Left **Midland Red's motorway coaches were technically advanced – and capable of high speeds. They were an overwhelming success, boosting ridership between Birmingham and London with journey times almost half those achieved by pre-motorway services. The route boards above the side windows harked back to an earlier era – but these were thoroughly modern coaches. Note the driver's white-topped hat in this view at Victoria Coach Station in 1963.**
Iain MacGregor

Left **Midland Red's motorway coaches were technically advanced – and capable of high speeds. They were an overwhelming success, boosting ridership between Birmingham and London with journey times almost half those achieved by pre-motorway services. The route boards above the side windows harked back to an earlier era – but these were thoroughly modern coaches. Note the driver's white-topped hat in this view at Victoria Coach Station in 1963.**
Iain MacGregor

Below **London's Victoria Coach Station was a busy place in the 1960s, with coaches departing for all four corners of Britain. An ECW-bodied Bristol of United Auto loads for the journey north, its boot already filling up. The use of a rear destination display was extremely unusual on coaches. This section of Victoria Coach Station has long since been roofed over.**
John Aldridge

vidualistic of BET fleets – the Birmingham & Midland Motor Omnibus Company, to give Midland Red its full title. BMMO was BET's biggest subsidiary, with a fleet of 1,900 buses and coaches, and it was unique in that it built its own vehicles. It had been a pioneer in the exploration of alternative driveline layouts, producing experimental rear-engined chassis in the mid-1930s, some of which were rebuilt with mid-mounted engines during World War II. The outcome of this was the production by BMMO of underfloor-engined single-deckers from 1946.

These included coach models, and in 1958 a prototype of a new C5 coach was built. This was based on the company's S14 bus, which used a BMMO-built 8-litre engine in an integral steel structure which had such advanced features as servo-assisted hydraulically-operated disc brakes all round and independent front suspension. The C5 featured rubber-metal suspension in place of the leaf springs fitted to coaches of the period. However much the drivers appreciated these luxuries, they were still faced with a constant-mesh gearbox – a five-speed overdrive unit. The prototype weighed 6 tons 9 cwt 1 qr,

which was about the norm for a 30ft-long underfloor-engined coach of the time.

The C5 was a front-entrance 37-seater (hitherto all Midland Red coaches had been of centre entrance layout) and to meet the requirements of motorway operation it was developed as the CM5 with a high-ratio rear axle and a turbocharged engine, which increased power output from 104 to 135bhp. CM5s were used to inaugurate the Birmingham to London motorway express service when the first stretch of the M1 motorway was opened in November 1959. They were able to run at speeds in excess of 80mph, at a time when coaches on all roads other than motorways were still legally restricted to an archaic 30mph. On tests at the Motor Industry Research Association's track at Nuneaton a CM5 reached 85mph. High-speed testing showed that the most noticeable wind noise was being created by the hinges on the entrance door; these were streamlined slightly, which cut the noise. High speed running also caused the wiper blades to lift away from the windscreen. This was remedied by simply increasing the strength of the wiper arm springs.

Tyres, not surprisingly, were an area which needed careful examination on a vehicle grossing 10 tons and running at much higher speeds than any previous British coach. Midland Red tried some 15 different types and makes of tyre, and increased the size of the front tyres from the original 9.00x20 12-ply to 10.00x20 14-ply.

The styling was distinctive, with a six-piece flat-glass lantern-type windscreen and shallow side windows which betrayed this remarkable vehicle's origins in the humble S14 bus. Unusually the roof, including front and rear domes, was a single glass-fibre moulding. The C5 family of coaches ran in Midland Red's smart coach livery, red with a black roof. It is an indication of the high profile achieved by Midland Red with its motorway coaches that although quite untypical of coaches of the period they were chosen as a subject to be modelled by Corgi Toys.

Once in service the coaches were fitted with windscreen washers to cope with the amount of dirt being thrown up in winter. There were also problems with the amount of water which lay on the motorway surface and some vulnerable items were wrapped in polythene. At speed the drain holes in the rear boot drew in water and air. To overcome this the company tried pressurising the boot by fitting a small centrifugal fan.

Before launching its motorway service, Midland Red approached the Ministry of Transport in the spring of 1959 seeking permission to run 45ft-long 60-seat coaches. The answer was in the negative.

Despite this – and despite limits on the number of duplicates which could be run – the service was an instant success. In November 1958 Midland Red's Birmingham to London coaches using the pre-motorway route carried just 722 people. In November 1959 the new motorway service carried 6,496 passengers and the company was turning would-be travellers away. The return fare was just £1 1s 3d – compared with £2 2s for travel by British Railways.

The opening of motorways often led to the introduction of new services, rather than the simple re-routeing of existing ones. And when seen against the background of the severe cuts being made to the rail network in the early 1960s, coaches were increasingly providing the main links between many smaller towns for those without cars. By 1965 Midland Red's ME1 service between Birmingham and London was running three times daily, with a scheduled time of 2 hours 55 minutes. It's a tribute to the CM5 – and a comment on the chronic overcrowding that would later characterise Britain's motorways – that 30 years later National Express had shaved just five minutes off this time. (Although, of course, coaches in the late 1990s also have speed limiters fitted and are banned from using the outside lane of the motorway.) In 1965 there was still a slow service to Birmingham using the A5 and serving Coventry on route, which took an incredible 5 hours 16 minutes to get from the capital to the second city of the Empire.

While Midland Red's high-profile service attracted most attention in the early days of motorway operation, it did have a rival in its claim to be the first coach service to use the M1. The other claimant was Birch Bros, the old-established London coach operator, which introduced a Bedford to Kings Cross service via the motorway on 2nd November 1959, as an alternative to its established A-road route.

Leyland was alive to the possibilities which the motorway network would open up, and of the unsuitability of its small-engined and relatively noisy Tiger Cub for comfortable high-speed cruising. The result was the announcement in 1959 of the new Leopard chassis, in effect a Tiger Cub with Leyland's more powerful O.600 engine – last seen in coaches in the Royal Tiger in the early part of the decade. The Leopard was launched at the 1959 Scottish Motor Show

30ft and 36ft models ...

powerful ... economical ... low–weight bus & coach chassis

MOTORWAY EXPRESS

London Bedford Rushden

Express Service 203M

✳

NONSTOP between WESTONING and LONDON via Motorway M1

Saturday 1 May 1965 to Friday 31 Dec. 1965

or until further notice

BIRCH BROS. LTD

and was soon to be a popular choice with large coach operators. The coach version, the L2, had a 130bhp engine rating and the option of an Eaton two-speed axle. One of the first orders, and a prestigious one at that, came from Western SMT which took 20 with Alexander bodies for operation on its Glasgow to London service. These used one of the standard Alexander coach body shells of the period, the design introduced in 1953 which had a gently curved waistline. Most coaches of this type were 41-seaters, while Western's Leopards had just 30 reclining seats and a toilet compartment. They ran on the London service for six years, after which most were sold to Ulsterbus.

Other early Leopard users included the Sheffield Joint Omnibus Committee, which specified Weymann's relatively rare Fanfare body on 14, Lewis Cronshaw of Hendon, Ellen Smith of Rochdale, Wallace Arnold, and two Glasgow operators, McDowall's and Cotters. In the late 1950s and early 1960s independents were still firmly wedded to lightweights and however good Leyland's new Leopard was, it sold in relatively small numbers to small operators, with 24 in 1963 being the highest annual figure at this time.

The arrival of the Leopard effectively killed the Tiger Cub as a coach chassis. The Leopard was altogether more suitable for long-distance running, and very few Tiger Cubs were pur-

Right **Duple's body for the Thames PSV was basically the Super Vega with different grille treatment. York Bros of Northampton, whose coach fleet around this period was 100 per cent Duple, operated this Thames, complete with antimacassars on the headrests. At this stage the body was un-named.** *Capital Transport*

Below **The classic Duple Super Vega was restyled for 1959. It was higher than the previous range and was produced for two seasons in this style with two-piece windscreen. The top-sliding windows were an option (drop-down windows were standard). The side mouldings were now described as the "J" style. A smart Gold Line Bedford SB waits for custom at Dunoon in 1962.** *Iain MacGregor*

The original Crusader from Harrington was a good-looking body, apart perhaps from the front. The main side windows on this 1959 Crusader give a hint of the new look which would appear with the Cavalier. The operator was Orange Luxury Coaches of Brixton, which had been part of the George Ewer group of companies since 1953.
Stephen Barber collection

chased for coach use after 1961. A notable exception was Alexander (Midland), which bought Tiger Cubs for private hire and tour work until 1964, and Trent which took a batch of eight in 1965. The Tiger Cub coach finally faded from the scene in 1968, by which time annual deliveries were down to single figures. From 1962 the original PSUC1/2 coach variant of the Tiger Cub was supplanted by the PSUC1/12 which had Leyland's O.400 Power-Plus engine rated at 131bhp in place of the 108bhp O.350.

Also appearing in 1959 was a new coach of a rather different type: the Thames Trader. Bedford's simple SB had been a best-seller with small independents since its launch in 1950. By 1959 the vast majority were SB1s with Bedford's 300 cu in (4.9-litre) diesel engine, although a petrol engine of the same size remained an option in the SB3 which was specified by a decreasing minority of operators. The noisy diesel was rated at 97bhp; the quiet petrol at a livelier 133bhp. There was a Perkins diesel option too. It is a measure of Bedford's popularity that in 1959 Bedford chassis accounted for 67 per cent of Plaxton's output.

The SB had much in common with Bedford's S-series truck range, and rival light truck maker Ford took a leaf out of the Dunstable manufacturer's book when it unveiled in the spring of 1957 a prototype Thames Trader PSV with a Duple body. Like the SB the Thames Trader had a front mounted engine and was designed to accommodate 41-seat 30ft-long bodywork with an entrance immediately behind the front axle. The Trader's engine, Ford-built of course, was a 100bhp 5.42-litre diesel unit. Petrol power was offered as an option, but was rare indeed in a Thames. By the end of the 1950s diesel reigned supreme and very few coach operators were buying new petrol-powered vehicles.

Salopia Saloon Coaches of Whitchurch, Shropshire, was one of very few operators still buying petrol-engined coaches – Bedford SBs. Salopia argued that with an average annual mileage of between 18,000 and 20,000 for its coaches it could afford the heavy fuel consumption – 9 or 10mpg compared with 16 to 18mpg for a diesel-engined SB. Petrol-engined coaches were also cheaper to buy.

The Thames Trader PSV was in series production in time for the 1959 coaching season and was soon giving Bedford a run for its money

in the lightweight sector of the coach market. The Thames generally had bodywork by Burlingham, Duple or Plaxton, although some were also bodied by Harrington and Yeates. Duple offered a revised body, which was in effect a modernised Super Vega with a slightly more upright front profile and a higher build overall, while Plaxton's body was the Consort.

To publicise the new model a Duple-bodied demonstrator ran a trip from London to Moscow, before appearing in the demonstration park at the 1959 Scottish Motor Show, alongside two other coaches with Harrington Crusader and Burlingham's new Seagull 60 bodywork. However, where big bus fleets needed lightweight coaches they initially tended to remain loyal to Bedford. An early exception to this generalisation was BET's East Kent subsidiary, which took one Thames, with Harrington bodywork, in 1960. This was a Crusader, a model introduced in 1958 on Bedford SB chassis. The original Crusader had twin flat glass windscreens flanked by curved corner sections. For 1960 it was updated with a new front end with a stylish two-piece curved screen.

The Thames was a bit heavier than the Bedford SB, typically weighing around 5 tons 4 cwt 2 qrs with a Duple body, at a time when

Every ride a joy ride...
for passengers and operators alike!

Coachwork by 'Duple'.

THE COMMER 'AVENGER' coach is the finest value for money on the market to-day. LOOK AT THESE OUTSTANDING FEATURES: Ample room for 41 passengers in full 8 ft. wide coachwork; fully-proved suspension to ensure superb comfort on the longest journeys; smooth power and exceptional economy from the phenomenal Rootes diesel engine—many operators report fuel consumptions of 20 m.p.g.—driver comfort and safety assured by well-positioned controls, light and accurate in action; and powerful vacuum servo-operated brakes. Commer overdrive can also be fitted as an optional extra.
Your local dealer will give you full details.

COUPLED WITH THE ECONOMY OF THE ROOTES DIESEL ENGINE

COMMER 'AVENGER'
41 SEAT COACH
❋ BACKED BY ROOTES COUNTRY-WIDE PARTS AND SERVICE ORGANISATION ❋

A ROOTES PRODUCT—BUILT STRONGER TO LAST LONGER!

COMMER CARS LTD. LUTON BEDFORDSHIRE
BUS & COACH. April 1962
EXPORT DIVISION: ROOTES LTD. DEVONSHIRE HOUSE PICCADILLY LONDON W I

5

Left **By the start of the 1960s, Commer Avenger sales – always well below those of Bedford – were falling off dramatically, helped by the growing popularity of the Thames PSV. This Avenger IV was new in 1960 to Moore of Kelvedon and had a 41-seat Yeates body, set high to clear the Commer's engine. Most Commers had high-set bodywork, but seldom quite as ungainly as this. The Moore business was taken over by Eastern National in 1963, in whose ownership the coach is seen leaving London Victoria for Jaywick Sands. Despite being a distinct oddball in a Tilling fleet, it served Eastern National until 1968.** *John Aldridge*

Below **ECW wasn't the only coachbuilder in Lowestoft. Rather less well-known, and much less prolific, was Belle Coach Works which was owned by local coach operator Shreeve. Tourist Coaches was one of Shreeve's trading names, as seen on this Belle-bodied Bedford SB of 1963. The last Belle body was built in 1964.** *D N Warren*

Right **A unique style of Alexander body was built on ten Albion Nimbuses, delivered in 1960 to the Alexander and Lawson fleets. All ten were taken over by Alexander (Midland) in 1961, as seen here in Glasgow's Dundas Street bus station. They were used for day excursions and Highland holiday tours. The first was an exhibit at the 1959 Scottish Motor Show, but failed to generate much interest for chassis or body. These pretty little coaches were withdrawn in 1970.** *Harry Hay*

the comparable SB/Super Vega combination tipped the scales at around 4 tons 18 cwt 3 qrs. But both were remarkably low figures for a 41-seat coach. From the passengers' viewpoint there was little to choose between them. Having the engine in the saloon meant that they were noisy, particularly for those travelling near the front. Ride quality, too, was generally inferior to mid-engined models.

The Duple Super Vega on the Bedford SB and the similar body offered on the Thames and the Commer were restyled for 1959. This heavier-looking body style was also adopted for an improved Britannia range on mid-engined chassis. There was less of a sweep down towards the rear on the waistline, and the new body incorporated double-curvature windscreens. The Loughborough-built Donington also received curved screens.

The arrival of the Thames Trader psv chassis finally put an end to what had previously been Bedford's only rival in lightweight coaches, Commer. The Commer Avenger used a 105bhp Rootes three-cylinder two-stroke TS3 diesel engine and was usually bodied by Duple or Plaxton, albeit in fairly small numbers. Commer advertising claimed fuel consumption figures of up to 20mpg.

The last major user of the Avenger was Southdown which took 15 with Burlingham bodies in 1959 followed by a further 30 with Harrington bodies in 1960/62. The Avenger made its last Commercial Motor Show appearance at Earls Court in 1960, with a Yeates-bodied vehicle for Simonds of Botesdale. It would continue to sell in small numbers until 1964 when Commer finally threw in the towel. The last Duple-bodied Commers were built in 1961, the last Commer to be bodied by Yeates was completed in 1962. Plaxton bodied three Commers in 1963 and one, the last, in 1964. This went to Moss Motor Tours on the Isle of Wight.

One fairly late Commer, supplied to McLennan of Spittalfield in 1960, was unusual in having a coach body built in the operator's own body shop. Such examples of operator-built bodywork were rare by this period. The only other small operator with in-house body-building capabilities at this time was Shreeve of Lowestoft whose Belle Coach Works built very small numbers of bodies, finishing in 1964 with a 37-seater on a Bedford SB.

Another chassis maker to give up on coaches was Dennis. The company's front-engined Lancet had enjoyed brief popularity in the late 1940s, but its underfloor-engined successor, introduced in 1955, had fared less well. East Kent was the biggest user with 30, followed by Glenton Tours of London, which took nine with Plaxton bodies, including the last, which entered service in 1961. In all Dennis built just 49 mid-engined Lancet coaches.

Operators of small coaches were hardly spoilt for choice at the end of the 1950s. With the demise of the Bedford OB in 1951 there had been no strong contenders in this market for a coach offering around 29 seats. One model which was available was the Albion Nimbus, powered by a four-cylinder version of Leyland's six-cylinder horizontal O.350 engine as fitted to the Tiger Cub. The biggest fleet of Nimbus coaches was run by Scottish Omnibuses Group subsidiary W Alexander & Sons, with some being allocated to the associated Lawson's business: they had 15 between them. All had Alexander bodies, the later vehicles being as stylish as the early ones had been plain, as Alexander made full use of the opportunities afforded by glass fibre to add style to its body designs. Highland Omnibuses also ran Nimbuses with Alexander coach bodies of the early design. Smiths of Wigan ran a few Nimbuses with Plaxton bodies, which it bought primarily for operation on tours to the Scottish Highlands.

Bedford still had a presence in this sector of the market with the truck-derived 4-ton C4Z and 5-ton C5Z, offered with the choice of petrol or diesel engines. They were generally supplied with either Bedford's 3.52-litre petrol engine or 4.93-litre diesel, indicated by the suffix 1 or 2 respectively – for example C4Z1. Most were bodied with a scaled-down version of Duple's Super Vega body, which revived the Vista name, as previously used for the classic Duple body on the Bedford OB. MacBrayne was the biggest single user of the C-type Bedford, taking 22 between 1958 and 1961, but a number were supplied to small operators throughout the country. From 1959 Duple called its small body the Super Vista.

Tel. Ryde 4025

MOSS

WHITE HEATHER

LUXURY COACHES

The best way of seeing this lovely Island—many different tours for all-day, half-day and evening

Book on the coach or at our office:

1 THE ESPLANADE, RYDE

PRIVATE PARTIES CATERED FOR

Left **The associated Western National and Southern National companies were the biggest users of the Bristol SU. All SU coaches had this style of ECW body. This is a 33-seater on the long-wheelbase SUL4A chassis and dates from 1962. It and other similar coaches in the Western National fleet were ultimately downgraded to bus work.** *Colin Brown*

Below **Burlingham's classic Seagull on a Ribble Leyland Tiger Cub. Originally designed with a centre entrance – hence the short bay in mid-wheelbase – Burlingham cleverly adapted it to front entrance without compromising the body's smooth lines. The roof-mounted destination box was not a standard fitting, but the flat-glass windscreens were used for many later Seagull bodies. This is a 1956 coach on an excursion. It had a 10-year life with Ribble.** *Frank Mussett*

Right **Valliant of Ealing bought panoramic-windowed Seagulls in 1959. These soon had extra glazing bars added, dividing each of the big side windows into two smaller ones. The polished moulding at wheelarch level was a feature of the big-windowed Mk VII Seagulls.** *Stephen Barber collection*

For Tilling group companies needing a small coach there was the Bristol SU. Available in two wheelbases, the 12ft 6in SUS and the 15ft SUL, the SU used the 4.1-litre Albion EN250 engine which powered the Nimbus and which could provide fuel economy in the region of 16mpg. Most Bristol SUs went to the Southern and Western National companies, and these included 36 SUL4A models fitted with 33-seat ECW coach bodies. The only other SU coaches were a pair for United Welsh. Production of the SU ceased in 1966.

In 1960 Duple made the move which would underpin its position as Britain's biggest coach builder with the take-over of Burlingham of Blackpool for the sum of £550,000. Burlingham had been building bodies since 1928 and in postwar years had achieved widespread popularity with its attractive Seagull body which took its name from the first operator to buy one, local firm Seagull Coaches.

The Seagull, launched in 1950, was a classic, and could be found in many well-known fleets. One of the biggest users was Ribble, which took almost 100 on Royal Tiger and Tiger Cub chassis between 1953 and 1958. Wallace Arnold was

another major user, with Seagull bodies on AEC and Leyland chassis, and one on a Sentinel, a marque for which the company was briefly a sales agent.

This popular body underwent a number of changes during its 10-year production life. Initially launched with a centre entrance, a front-entrance version was added in 1954. Revised glazing in 1957 saw the adoption of window pans, primarily for a Ribble order, which spoiled the crisp appearance of the original design, while at the 1958 Commercial Motor Show a panoramic-windowed version – the Mark VII – was announced, aping Plaxton's Panorama. By this time the Seagull had perhaps outlived its usefulness, and this final variant was built in small numbers. Buyers of panoramic-windowed Seagulls included two London operators – Banfield and Valliant, plus Blue Bus of Willington and Yelloway of Rochdale. The body structure of the Mark VII Seagull proved to have been inadequately developed and some were rebuilt later in their lives with the missing window pillars reinstated, to restore their structural integrity.

With the Show Mark VII, for Seagull Coaches

of Blackpool, Burlingham tried taking glass fibre a step further than its competitors by using glass fibre panelling, which was to be colour-impregnated to eliminate the need for repainting. However, to achieve an acceptable finish it still had to be painted, and so the idea was abandoned.

For front-engined chassis there was a range of Seagull derivatives, none of which had quite the style of the original body designed for mid-engined chassis. The final version of this, in 1959, was offered on Thames and Bedford chassis and was a bizarre amalgam of early 1950s styling for the sides married to somewhat futuristic-looking wrap-round windscreens.

When Duple took over, Burlingham was building around 300 bodies a year, mainly on lightweight chassis, and was in the throes of change. The original Seagull was being replaced in 1960 by a new range, the Seagull 60 for front-engined chassis and the Seagull 70 for under-floor-engined types. Both were attractive bodies with some shared styling cues. The grille treatment was slightly different depending on whether the body was mounted on a Thames or a Bedford chassis.

Above **The sophistication of the original Seagull was lost when a restyled variant was made available for Thames and Bedford chassis in 1959. The side elevation retains the old Burlingham style, but the front was not one of the company's better designs. Fountain Coaches of Twickenham was the original owner of this Bedford SB1. It was bought by Docherty of Irvine, a member of the A1 group, in 1962. The blanking plate over the lower section of the grille has been added by the operator, suggesting some dissatisfaction with the Bedford's heaters.** *Iain MacGregor*

Left **In 1960 Burlingham produced a much more stylish body for Bedfords and Fords, the Seagull 60, here seen on a Bedford owned by Imperial of Windsor but running on hire to another Berkshire operator, Carter of Maidenhead. The basic body style would remain in production until 1963, by which time it would have evolved into the Gannett.** *D N Warren*

Above **Burlingham's Seagull 70 for mid-engined chassis was built in small numbers. Scottish Omnibuses, with 11 on AEC Reliance chassis, was the biggest user. The coach visible on the right shows the rear-end styling of the Burlingham Seagull 60, 61 and 70 family of bodies. Note how the Scottish Omnibuses name is italicised backwards to fit the aperture of the offside destination display.** *Iain MacGregor*

Burlingham launched the Seagull 60 saying: "The original Seagull design of luxury coach was introduced in 1950, and has reigned supreme in a world of keen competition for 10 years. It is now our pleasure to introduce a worthy successor to this famous model with full confidence that it embodies, in design and construction, every modern characteristic that coach operators and travelling public alike expect from a Burlingham body."

The original Seagull 60 had the centre section of the roof raised slightly and glazed in translucent perspex for its full length; however this leaked and was soon deleted. Inadequate fixing could also cause some of the panels to fly off. The Seagull 70 was one of the first British coaches to have paired twin headlights – it was an idea imported from the USA and would be briefly fashionable.

But the new Seagulls were to be short-lived as Duple rationalised its range and Burlingham became Duple (Northern), adopting the title of a subsidiary operation set up by Duple in 1958 to handle sales and service in the north. Scottish Omnibuses opted for the rare Seagull 70 on AEC Reliance chassis for eleven 34-seat touring coaches purchased in 1961 and delivered in a distinctive cream and maroon livery instead of the standard cream and green. Unusually for Scottish Omnibuses coaches they were named, the names having connections with the novelist Sir Walter Scott. This echoed a practice used by SMT for Leyland Tiger coaches on its Edinburgh to London service in the 1930s. With Seagull 70 production barely reaching 50 units, Scottish Omnibuses was the biggest buyer of the type. Other well-known users included

BET subsidiaries East Midland, Sunderland District, Trent, Wakefields and Yorkshire Traction. The Trent coaches had non-standard rubber-mounted windows.

In 1960 Duple was building quite a variety of coaches, at a time when there was still much bespoke production to meet the needs of individual customers. The most standardised models were those built on front-engined Bedford, Thames and Commer chassis. On underfloor-engined chassis there was the Loughborough-built Donington and the Britannia – the latter built at Hendon and generally similar to the bodies on front-engined chassis but with neater frontal styling.

The Britannia was usually a front-entrance design, but a stylish centre entrance model was built too and had a more curvaceous front end with Super Vega windscreens. Users of the centre-entrance Britannia included Black & White Motorways, which took a batch of eight on AEC Reliance chassis in 1960. Similar coaches were supplied to Samuelson of London, whose fleet was 100 per cent Reliance/Duple at the start of the 1960s. On all Duple models

Left **The final version of the front-entrance Duple Britannia, in the fleet of Baxter of Airdrie. New in 1960, it was a 41-seater on an AEC Reliance chassis. The main body structure was similar to the more common Super Vega on the Bedford SB chassis, but with an upright front to accommodate the entrance door.** *Iain MacGregor*

except the Donington the large, curved, front screens were matched by a deep curved three-piece rear window in which the centre section formed the emergency exit.

The Donington was improved in 1961 with the option of bigger windows and longer bays, reducing from six to four the number of main side windows. Twin headlights were offered as an option. But it had a short life in this form and was withdrawn from production in 1962. In all, not far over 100 Doningtons of all types had been built.

Similarly the Super Vega, which was nearing the end of its production life, was given a new grille and a three-piece windscreen in place of the previous two-piece design. From the 1961 season and to coincide with the adoption of the new three-piece windscreen, the bodies on the Thames and the Commer were given names – Yeoman and Corinthian respectively. The Corinthian used the same new grille as the 1962 Super Vega, while the Yeoman carried forward the grille from the previous body style on the Thames chassis.

Duple's principal rival was Plaxton, based in Scarborough. The existence of major coach bodybuilders – Burlingham, Harrington, Plaxton – in seaside resorts reflected the traditional seasonality of coach manufacture. Most coach operators wanted their new coaches in the spring, which meant that production was at its peak in the winter months. As demand for coach bodies slackened, other types of jobs became available for workers who could find seasonal summer employment elsewhere before returning to coach building in the autumn. In 1961 Plaxton opened a new factory at Eastfield, on the outskirts of Scarborough. This was done to increase capacity; the existing factory in Seamer Road was retained.

Plaxton's range was rather more stable than Duple's. The striking Panorama has already been mentioned, and was available only on heavyweight chassis. Plaxton had in 1960 (for the 1961 season) replaced the Consort with the Embassy, although this was a case of evolution in design, rather than revolution. On Bedford and Thames chassis both models shared the same oval grille – a Plaxton design feature since the early 1950s – and the same gently sloping waistline. The Embassy had a different profile for the side pillars, with a slight angle inward from the waist, removing the rather slab-sided

Below left The centre-entrance Britannia had a much more rounded front profile and in this final version used the same three-piece windscreen as was fitted from 1961 to the Super Vega, Corinthian and Yeoman bodies on front-engined chassis. The grille incorporating the destination display was only used on 1962 Britannias – the model's last year. Oxfordshire company Charlton-on-Otmoor Services operated this Reliance, seen at their depot alongside a classic Fina diesel pump. *Paul Caudell*

This page top The Donington, built in Loughborough by Duple (Midland), was used on AEC Reliance chassis by MacBrayne for long-distance coach services and, as seen here by Loch Eck, on tours. This is a 1962 example – the last year of Donington production – and shows the large side windows used on the last Doningtons. The front grille is the same as that used on the Hendon-built Britannia. *Iain MacGregor*

This page bottom A new grille and three-piece windscreen were used to rejuvenate the Duple Super Vega body on the Bedford SB chassis in 1961. Hills of West Bromwich owned this example, seen parked outside St Pancras Station in London in the summer of 1963. The three-piece screen was also fitted to bodies on Thames and Commer chassis. *Capital Transport*

look of the Consort range. A more modern layout was used for the polished side mouldings.

In 1959 Bee Line of West Hartlepool had taken 17 new Bedford SBs from Plaxton, and six of those had the floor raised by 3½in to reduce engine intrusion, and the steering column repositioned so that it was almost vertical. This allowed the driving position to be moved forward, creating more space for the seats behind. On the new Embassy this raised floor was made a production option – known as the C-type – but it took a sharp eye to spot the difference between high- and low-built Embassy bodies.

There was also an Embassy body for midengined chassis, with different front end treatment depending on the position of the entrance. Front-entrance bodies had a fairly upright front, as used on the Panorama, while on centre-entrance bodies the front end was curved, not unlike Duple's centre-entrance Britannia. Mid-engined Embassy bodies used a smaller, more attractive grille than that fitted to front-engined models. The Consort name was retained for a 19/20-seat body fitted in small numbers to Bedford's little J2 truck-based chassis.

The Panorama was restyled at the same time, getting a much more modern look with a smaller grille and just a little curvature to the waist with the window line dipping slightly towards the rear. The Embassy body on lightweight chassis was revised in 1962 as the

Embassy II, the most obvious change being a fashionable peak to the front dome. This usually incorporated a destination display which was angled forward, although this item could be deleted which made the front dome look just a bit bare. This style of Embassy II was built on Bedford SB and on the Thames Trader, still in two slightly different heights.

But somewhat confusingly the Embassy body on mid-engined chassis – which didn't have the peaked dome – was also classed as the Embassy II. And to compound the confusion, the centre-entrance Panorama was called the Embassy. Plaxton's brochure, perhaps taking a swipe at the variety emanating from Duple's factories, said that the company's designers had "avoided the tricks and frills of fashion that date so quickly, and presented a graceful, elegant luxury coach in the fine Plaxton tradition".

The Panorama had been selling to Plaxton's traditional customers, the independents, but from 1962 it started to win company orders from BET group subsidiaries other than Sheffield United. The first were for East Midland, Midland Red, North Western, Potteries, Yorkshire Traction and Yorkshire Woollen, along with Black & White and Timpson in which BET had an interest.

Although overshadowed by Duple and Plaxton, Harrington had built up a steady following during the 1950s, and took a giant step forward at the start of 1960 with the launch of its crisply-styled Cavalier, replacing the rather frumpy Wayfarer. The Cavalier had almost rakish styling – in keeping with its name – and was built on mid-engined AEC and Leyland chassis. It immediately won orders for 47 from six BET subsidiaries – East Yorkshire, Greenslades, Hebble, Northern General, South Wales Transport and Yorkshire Woollen, plus BET-associated Timpson. A novel feature of the Cavalier was the use of side flaps which lifted parallel to the body on a pantograph, rather than being hinged at the top. This made it easier to open them in confined spaces, and the idea was later adopted for the boot door too.

Bedford launched the definitive 1960s small coach in September 1961 with the announcement of the new VAS, which replaced the C4 and C5. The new small Bedford was most commonly found in diesel-engined VAS1 form, with Bedford's six-cylinder 97bhp unit; the VAS2 (later succeeded by the bigger-engined VAS3) was the petrol-engined alternative. The engine was mounted over the front axle, as on the C4 and C5, with the entrance behind the front wheel. Among the features setting the VAS apart from the previous generation of small Bedfords was the fitment of air brakes to the VAS1, which gave a characteristic whistling sound when applied. The VAS2 and VAS3 retained vacuum brakes. Four- or five-speed gearboxes were on

Left **Hardwick of Eston, Middlesbrough, operated four coaches – all Bedford SBs with Plaxton bodies. This 1961 SB1 shows the Embassy body with the added embellishment of SUT-style mouldings.** *Capital Transport*

Right above **One of the most attractive versions of Plaxton's Panorama was this 1961 30ft-long model, seen on an AEC Reliance owned by Shaw Bros of Byers Green, County Durham. Shaw operated six coaches at this time and the twin air horns and plastic flowers on the dashboard indicate an operator which took a pride in its fleet. The company was taken over by United Automobile in 1975.** *Capital Transport*

Right middle **Harrington's Wayfarer body, on an AEC Reliance operated by Maidstone & District. M & D took 20 similar coaches in 1960, followed by a further 20 in 1961. A travel-stained 1960 Wayfarer is seen arriving at London's Victoria Coach Station in 1970. Most of M & D's postwar coaches had Harrington bodies.** *Geoff Lumb*

Right below **The Harrington Cavalier marked a major step forward from the Wayfarer, and immediately won sizeable orders from BET group companies. These included Northern General, which took 10 Cavaliers on Leyland Leopard L2T chassis in 1961. These were 37-seat touring coaches. The T suffix on the chassis code indicated the fitment of a two-speed rear axle.** *Martin Llewellyn*

offer. The handbrake operated on the transmission, rather than on the wheels. The VAS had small 16in wheels, which kept the frame height low and helped minimise wheelarch intrusion.

Insofar as the British Coach Rally was a barometer of operators' preferences, the 1961 event attracted 23 Bedfords, 19 Fords, 19 AECs – and just three Leylands. A Duple-bodied Reliance from London-based Samuelson was the overall winner. The growing success of the British Coach Rally, which had started with Clacton-on-Sea as its venue in 1955 before moving to Brighton in 1956, prompted the organisation of a similar event in the North. This was held at Blackpool from 1961 and was known as the National Coach Rally, although in fact the two rallies were best known by their locations rather than by their official titles. The Blackpool event, organised by the Wigan and District Coach Operators Association, tended to attract mainly northern (and occasionally Scottish) fleets.

There was also a short-lived West of England Coach Rally, held for three years. The last one, in Paignton in 1960, attracted fewer than 12 entrants and the event quietly faded from the scene.

Bigger coaches

In 1961 the big news – in more ways than one – was a relaxation in the length limits, from 30ft to 36ft. AEC and Leyland were quick to respond with lengthened versions of their Leopard and Reliance chassis, and the coach builders came up with new bodies to suit. The extra length allowed 49 (or even 51) seats to be fitted into a coach. As well as sanctioning longer coaches, the government permitted faster coaches, raising the speed limit on open roads from the laughable and largely unenforced 30mph, to a slightly more generous 40mph. There was no speed limit on the few stretches of motorway then in use.

Plaxton claimed to be the first builder to complete a 36ft-long coach for UK operation, with a Panorama body on an AEC Reliance 470 chassis for Sheffield United Tours in October 1961. In the same year Plaxton's output crossed the 500 mark for the first time.

Early users of 36ft coaches on express services in 1962 included Grey-Green, who reckoned to be the first to use a 36ft coach on a regular daily service into London when it introduced an AEC Reliance 470 with Harrington Cavalier 36 body to its Ipswich route. Black & White Motorways was not far behind, with a batch of nine Plaxton-bodied Leyland Leopards

bought for use on the company's Cheltenham to London service.

From AEC, as well as the existing AH470 engine for the Reliance, there came the option of the bigger and more-powerful AH590. This was a horizontal version of an engine introduced in 1958. Of 9.6-litre capacity, it was rated at up to 153bhp offering a useful increase in power over the 112bhp AH470 and making the Reliance capable of 70mph. Most Reliance coaches of this period had ZF six-speed gearboxes. Air suspension was an option, with four air bags on each axle, but it was an option which few operators were prepared to try.

Below left Plaxton developed an elegant lengthened Panorama for fitment to 36ft-long AEC Reliance and Leyland Leopard chassis. PMT was an early user of 36ft-long coaches, taking five of these 48-seat Panoramas on Leyland's new PSU3/3 Leopard in 1962. *Iain MacGregor*

Right For a very short period in the early 1960s Ford promoted mock wood panelling on its Cortina estate car. Someone at Sheffield United must have been impressed, and at the 1963 Blackpool coach rally the company entered this 36ft Reliance/Plaxton with part of the exterior panelling covered in wood-effect Arborite. This coach had been a Plaxton exhibit at the 1962 Commercial Motor Show. *Michael Fowler*

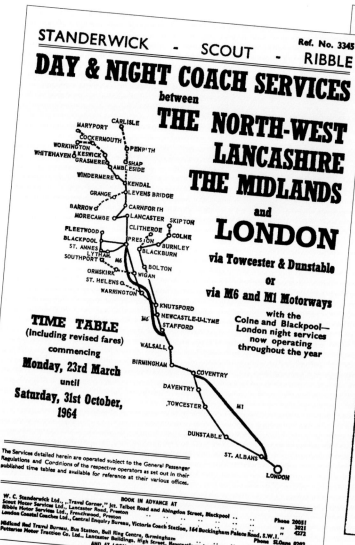

STANDERWICK - SCOUT - RIBBLE

Ref. No. 3345

DAY & NIGHT COACH SERVICES

between

THE NORTH-WEST LANCASHIRE THE MIDLANDS and LONDON

via Towcester & Dunstable

or

via M6 and M1 Motorways

with the Colne and Blackpool—London night services now operating throughout the year

TIME TABLE
(including revised fares)
commencing
Monday, 23rd March
until
Saturday, 31st October, 1964

The Services detailed herein are operated subject to the General Passenger Regulations and Conditions of the respective operators as set out in their published time tables and available for reference at their various offices.

BOOK IN ADVANCE AT

W. C. Standerwick Ltd., "Travel Corner," Jct. Talbot Road and Abingdon Street, Blackpool ..   **Phone 20051**
Scout Motor Services Ltd., Lancaster Road, Preston ..   **3021**
Ribble Motor Services Ltd., Frenchwood, Preston ..   **4272**
London Coastal Coaches Ltd., Central Enquiry Bureau, Victoria Coach Station, 164 Buckingham Palace Road, S.W.1 ..   **Phone SLOane 0202**
Midland Red Travel Bureau, Bus Station, Bull Ring Centre, Birmingham   **MID 4481**
Potteries Motor Traction Co. Ltd., Lancaster Buildings, High Street, Newcastle-under-Lyme   **65127**

AND AT LOCAL OFFICES AND AGENCIES

mb 80m 3/64

16

1964 EASY WAY HOLIDAYS

for any number of days

AT POPULAR RESORTS in all parts of Britain

★ FROM THE NORTH-WEST

SPECIMEN INCLUSIVE CHARGES FROM PRESTON

EIGHT DAYS HOLIDAY AT	Without Excursions	With Excursions
	£ s. d.	£ s. d.
BOURNEMOUTH	16 2 6	18 14 6
TORQUAY	17 13 6	19 11 6
CHELTENHAM	15 9 3	16 9 3
EDINBURGH	15 14 0	17 6 0

★ FROM THE MIDLANDS

SPECIMEN INCLUSIVE CHARGES FROM BIRMINGHAM

EIGHT DAYS HOLIDAY AT	Without Excursions	With Excursions
	£ s. d.	£ s. d.
SOUTHPORT	12 2 9	14 5 9
BLACKPOOL	12 18 3	14 13 0
MORECAMBE	11 13 6	13 5 0
AMBLESIDE	14 5 6	15 15 0
KESWICK	13 4 6	14 13 6

EASY WAY HOLIDAYS include

★ **Express travel** on Coach Services to and from the chosen resort. Go any day — come back any day.
★ **Good private hotel** accommodation with full board and staff gratuities.
★ **The reservation of seats** on sight-seeing excursions from the resort if required.

Full details and illustrated leaflets from :

W. C. Standerwick Ltd., "Travel Corner," Jct. Talbot Road and Abingdon Street, Blackpool. Phone 20051.
Scout Motor Services Ltd., Lancaster Road, Preston. Phone 3021.
Ribble Motor Services Ltd., Frenchwood, Preston. Phone 4272 or any Ribble Office.
Midland Red Travel Bureau, Bus Station, Bull Ring Centre, Birmingham. Phone MID 4481.
Potteries Motor Traction Co. Ltd., Lancaster Buildings, High Street, Newcastle-under-Lyme. Phone 65127.
London Coastal Coaches Ltd., Central Enquiry Bureau, Victoria Coach Station, 164 Buckingham Palace Road, S.W.1. Phone SLOane 0202.

Left top **Aldershot & District was one of two buyers of Park Royal coach bodies in the early 1960s. The body was the same as that supplied to East Kent, who similarly chose the AEC Reliance chassis, but with a simpler front panel, roof-mounted destination display and Auster opening windows of a design intended to reduce draughts. Aldershot & District took 15 of these coaches in 1962-63, primarily for operation on express services to London. Two are seen at a deserted Victoria Coach Station in 1963.** *Iain MacGregor*

Left bottom **This is the interior of a 1961 Plaxton Embassy and is typical of designs of the time. The glazed cove panels – an option on most coach bodies in the early 1960s – and the net luggage racks give a bright and airy appearance. The interior lights are located on the chrome strip which runs along the cantrail. This coach has additional glazing on the front and rear domes.** *Plaxton*

Below **Few multi-windowed 36ft Embassy bodies were built. Brewer's of Caerau operated this Reliance, bought new in 1962.** *Stephen Barber collection*

Barton Transport took delivery of six 36ft Reliances in 1962 with Yeates bodies. These were for operation on the company's established express service between Corby and Glasgow and for a new venture – a service from Nottingham to Warsaw. A return fare of £26 was charged for the 2,000-mile trip.

Deliveries to East Kent in 1962 included 20 Park Royal-bodied express coaches to the new maximum legal length. These were built on AEC's high-powered AH590-engined chassis and ran on services to London. They included vehicles in Europabus colours which operated the London to Dover leg of international services provided by Europabus. Similar coaches were supplied to Aldershot & District, albeit with a different style of front panel and the smaller AH470 engine. Later – post-1964 – versions of the body delivered to East Kent featured longer, fixed, side windows and forced-air ventilation. The last entered service in 1966.

Air suspension was also optional on the Leyland Leopard from 1961, both on the original L2 and on the new 36ft-long PSU3. One of the first air-suspended L2s, with centre-entrance Duple Britannia bodywork, was exhibited at the 1962 Commercial Motor Show at London's Earls Court and then sold to St Helens Transport. There was a slight weight penalty with air suspension. On an AEC Reliance, for example, it increased the chassis weight by 5cwt, although later in the decade as designs evolved Leyland could claim an increase in weight of just under 1cwt for air suspension on a Leopard. The first – and at this time – only fleet order for air-suspended coaches came from BET with orders for 65 L2 Leopards which went to Ribble (35, including 15 for the associated Standerwick fleet) and Southdown (30). All had Harrington Cavalier bodies.

The new PSU3 Leopard had an 18ft 6in wheelbase and used the same 125bhp O.600 engine as the L2. A choice of gearboxes was offered, the Leyland four-speed synchromesh in the PSU3/3R, and the four- or five-speed semi-automatic Pneumocyclic in the PSU3/4R. The Eaton two-

central entrance Plaxton Embassy II 49 seater
on AEC/Leyland II metre chassis

Above **Harrington's Grenadier had deeper windscreens and longer side windows and was offered in both 36ft-long and nominally 32ft-long versions. In 1964 Jones of Aberbeeg took two short Grenadiers – one on a Leopard, the other on the Reliance seen here in London – and one long Grenadier on a Leopard.** *Stewart J Brown*

Left **The only buyer of Weymann's 36ft-long Castilian body was Southdown which took two batches. The first five, delivered in 1962, were in effect multi-windowed Fanfares; one is seen pulling away from Victoria Coach Station. The following 15 in 1963 had panoramic windows, as illustrated on page 111. All were on Leyland Leopard chassis.** *Stewart J Brown*

Right above **Devon General's coach fleet traded as Grey Cars. New in 1962 were five AEC Reliances with Willowbrook's short-lived Viscount body. The reverse-rake rear window copied the style of Ford's contemporary Anglia saloon.**
Stewart J Brown collection

speed axle remained an option. The first PSU3s to enter service were those mentioned above for Black & White Motorways. In 1962 a PSU3/3R coach chassis was listed by Leyland at £2,790, which was just £99 more than the 30ft-long L2 and £315 – 13 per cent – more than the lighter PSUC1/12 Tiger Cub coach chassis.

For the new generation of 36ft-long coaches Plaxton not only came up with lengthened versions of its Panorama but also, less successfully, its multi-windowed Embassy, few of which were built. Harrington produced a lengthened Cavalier, as well as the Grenadier, which had longer fixed windows and a different style of front dash panel with a deeper windscreen – although the distinction between Grenadiers and Cavaliers soon became blurred, and short-length Grenadiers were produced, while some Cavaliers incorporated the Grenadier front panel. Even Weymann produced a lengthened Fanfare – the Castilian – initially with short bays, but later with panoramic windows. The only buyer was Southdown, which took delivery of 20 in 1962-63.

Willowbrook replaced its Viking in 1961 with

the Viscount, offering buyers a choice of rear-end styles. One was fairly conventional, the other had a Ford Anglia-style reverse-rake window, described in contemporary Duple publicity as a "cutaway back". Neither sold in any quantity, with total production totalling fewer than 30 bodies. BET subsidiary Devon General took 18 on two batches of Reliances in Grey Cars colours in 1961 and 1962. Four went to London independent Birch Bros for use on the company's Bedford to London motorway service. The Viscount name would be revived by Duple in the middle of the decade.

Duple came out with a totally new model for 1962, the metal-framed Continental, designed in Blackpool by the Burlingham team for fitment to 36ft-long chassis – although the prototype was actually put together by Duple (Midland) at Loughborough. This impressive-looking coach had a higher floor line than any previous Duple model, primarily to reduce wheelarch intrusion. This made the Continental 10ft 5in high at a time when 10ft was the norm. For 1963 there came the Alpine Continental, which featured deeper and longer fixed windows and forced-air

ventilation, as an alternative to the standard model with its top-sliding window vents (although to further confuse the situation some Continentals had fixed windows – including a few for Ribble).

The only other change of note was a revised grille, introduced in 1964, to give an improved flow of air to the radiator and thus counteract cooling problems, particularly on the AEC Reliance, a model which was widely recognised as being prone to overheating. The whole range lasted four years during which time 122 were produced at the Blackpool factory of Duple (Northern). It was built on AEC Reliance and Leyland Leopard PSU3 chassis, generally as a 49 or 51 seater. A 32ft version was on the drawing board but never reached production.

Also being built at Blackpool was a new body for the Bedford SB and Thames Trader, the quaintly named Gannet which followed the sea bird theme set by the Seagull. It was in fact little more than a facelifted Burlingham Seagull 61 – which was the Seagull 60 with a new grille. There was also a Seagull 62 listed, which differed from the Seagull 61 only in minor trim

Bottom left **Duple's Continental and Alpine Continental were striking high-floor designs built at the Blackpool factory of Duple (Northern) and offered on 36ft-long Leyland Leopard and AEC Reliance chassis. The Alpine Continental, seen here, featured longer windows and forced-air ventilation but was only produced for one season. This is a Leopard in the Stratford Blue fleet.**
Iain MacGregor

For Continental touring—one of the first 36 ft. luxury coaches to be built in Britain.

36ft. A.E.C. RELIANCE...
new profit opportunities for the new season

Since 1955 the "Reliance" has taken the honours in every important Coach Rally. And now the 36ft. model, entering its first summer season on the roads, adds *extra profitability* to performance and reliability by its enhanced seating capacity and even greater degree of comfort.

A.E.C. LIMITED
SOUTHALL
MIDDLESEX

detail. To further compound the confusion it would appear that there had been thoughts of using the Seagull 62 name for the Gannet, as the first artist's impression of the Gannet carried the Seagull 62 name. In any event, the Gannet had a three-piece windscreen where the Seagull 61 and Seagull 62 had two-piece screens. It also used Duple-designed seats, in place of Burlingham's Oyster seat, which had been fitted to the Seagull models, and it dispensed with the troublesome raised centre roof section of the models it replaced.

Burlingham's publicity described the Gannet as "a coach with a future". Its future was a short one. It lasted just one season and was superseded at the end of 1962 for the 1963 season by the altogether more attractive Duple-badged Firefly (originally described as the Seagull 63, but renamed before its launch), which was sold until 1965 alongside a new Hendon-built range of bodies. The only noteworthy change in the Firefly body was the adoption of simplified side mouldings in 1965.

An unusual feature of the Firefly was the use of interchangeable front and rear windows, a design feature which coach builders would latch on to with some enthusiasm in the 1960s. The idea was that in the event of the windscreen being broken it could be temporarily replaced by the rear window, allowing the coach to complete its journey with the minimum of discomfort to its passengers. In practice it wasn't such a good idea. Assuming someone could be found who had the skill to remove the back window and refit it in the front without damaging it, the airflow round the rear of a moving coach ensured a high level of discomfort for any passengers seated near the back.

The Firefly was also offered on a new lightweight chassis, the Albion Victor VT21L. Albion had been making staid and solid Victors since, it seemed, the dawn of the motoring age. The postwar Victor was a robust truck chassis which was used in a limited way for bus and coach applications (mainly in Africa, although also in small numbers in Britain with the FT39), but in 1962 Leyland decided to make a serious effort to win a share of the lightweight coach market, and its offering was the improved Victor VT21L, powered by a vertical O.370 engine mounted above the front axle – like the Bedford SB – and driving through an Albion five-speed constant-

Right **The Continental had shorter, opening windows, as illustrated on a 1965 Reliance operated by Dodds of Troon. This coach has the revised front adopted in 1964 which used some parts from the Firefly grille assembly. Alongside at Prestwick Airport stands a BOAC Reliance with Harrington Grenadier body, one of a pair used on a service to Glasgow city centre.** *Harry Hay*

mesh gearbox. It was a brave attempt, but coach operators stayed loyal to the market leaders and the Victor VT21L soon disappeared from Leyland's sales lists.

It sold for £1,686 in 1964 – or £1,706 for operators specifying the optional six-speed overdrive gearbox. Most Victors had Duple Firefly bodies, although a small number were bodied by Plaxton using the Embassy II body fitted to contemporary Bedfords and Thames Traders. Victors were bought by small fleets – although Wallace Arnold ran two for a short time. In all fewer than 100 were sold.

A 36ft-long version of the Firefly was also announced for 1963. Known as the Dragonfly it was unusual in being of centre-entrance design, by this time a very odd choice indeed which was favoured by just a handful of operators including Wallace Arnold and Glenton Tours of London. "The Dragonfly is destined to bring pride and pleasure to operators and passengers alike...", Duple enthused in its publicity. Only six were built. Four on AEC Reliance chassis were sold to London operator Samuelson, while the other two were Leyland Leopard demonstrators which were later bought by Fishwick of Leyland.

There were also plans to build the Firefly on standard 16ft 4in-wheelbase mid-engined chassis, in which form it would have had a centre entrance (like the Dragonfly) and been called the Kestrel.

This plethora of new products from Duple (Northern) reflected the difficulty of welding together two disparate operations. Duple was clearly reluctant to call a halt to design work which was in progress when it took over the Burlingham business, and the result was a confusion of new models in the first few years of the 1960s. But the development of a new range of

Middle right **Burlingham's Seagull 61 on a Thames Trader operated by Barrie of Balloch. The front grille was the only significant change from the Seagull 60. This body lasted just one season.** *Iain MacGregor*

Bottom Right **The Burlingham Gannett was a rework of the Seagull 61 with new windscreen and grille, and revised side mouldings. Some also had partially-enclosed rear wheels. The restyle could hardly be deemed an improvement. This smart Bedford SB was operated by Meadows of Preston, near Hitchin.** *Trevor Brookes*

Above The Duple Firefly, built in Blackpool, was introduced in 1962 for the 1963 season and was offered on the Thames Trader, Bedford SB and Albion Victor chassis. A Hanson of Huddersfield Thames takes part in the driving tests at the 1963 Blackpool coach rally. *Michael Fowler*

Left A minority of Albion Victor VT21L chassis had Plaxton Embassy bodies. The peaked dome distinguished the Embassy II from its predecessors, and normally housed a destination screen. The Embassy II was produced for just one season. New to Cox of Wallasey in 1963, this Victor had migrated north to Rennie of Dunfermline when photographed in Aberfeldy in 1970. *Iain MacGregor*

Above One of the least successful bodies to come out of the Blackpool factory of Duple (Northern) was the Dragonfly, of which only six were built. It was in essence a Firefly stretched to 11m. From the short bay behind the front wheel (which accommodated the entrance) to the rear the body was pure Firefly, with the extra length being incorporated in the bay above the front wheel. This Dragonfly was a Leyland demonstrator before joining the fleet of Fishwick of Leyland in whose ownership it is seen carrying a boisterous school party. *Trevor Brookes*

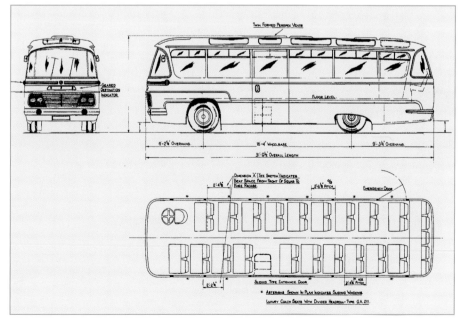

Right Duple had plans to build the Firefly on mid-engined chassis, in which form it was to have been called the Kestrel. None were built.

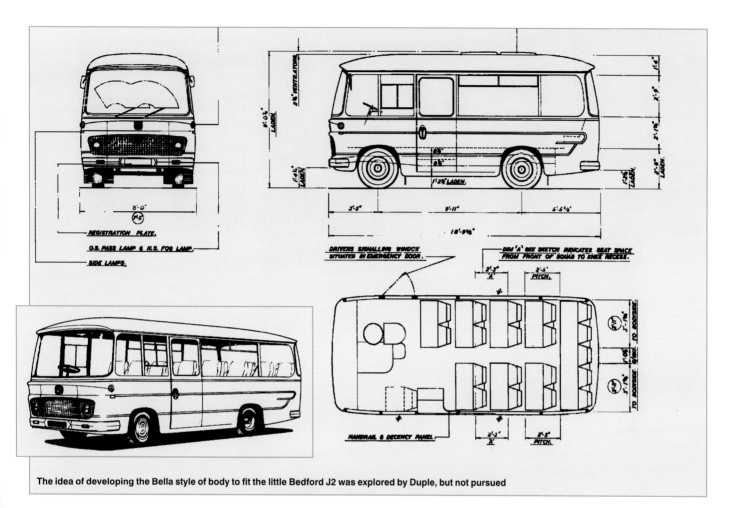

The idea of developing the Bella style of body to fit the little Bedford J2 was explored by Duple, but not pursued

Left above **The first of Duple's new Bella range was the little Bella Vista, available only on the Bedford VAS chassis, typically with 29 seats. The Scottish Bus Group was an early customer, taking 35 in 1962-63 which were shared between four of its subsidiaries. An Alexander (Midland) VAS1 is seen on a holiday coach tour on the Isle of Skye.** *Iain MacGregor*

Left below **The bigger Bella Vega was offered on the Bedford SB chassis. The same body when fitted to a Thames Trader was called the Trooper. The little flash above the rear wheel could be painted, as on this Leyland-engined SB8 owned by Hall Bros of South Shields or, at extra cost, have a fluted, polished, insert. Hall Bros was bought by Barton Transport in 1967.** *Capital Transport*

Right **This flashy body was a one-off by Marshall on a Thames 570E chassis. The hooded headlamps and peak over the windscreen place it firmly at the start of the '60s. The flash of colour on the side shows a hint of Yeates influence. It was new in the summer of 1962 and was operated by Miller Bros of Foxton, near Cambridge, until 1970.** *Geoff Mills*

Left **Harrington's Crusader II for Bedford and Thames chassis featured a restyled front, new two-piece windscreens and neater treatment of the side pillars in the area to the rear of the front wheelarch which combined to give the body an altogether fresher appearance. This example was delivered to Wilson of Glasgow. The appearance of the International Club falls somewhat short of the promise of its name.** *Iain MacGregor*

Right **The Crusader III from Harrington retained the frontal styling of the Mark II, but with bigger side windows which gave it a stronger family resemblance to the Cavalier. Eight Bedford SB5s with Crusader III bodies were purchased by Northern General in 1963. All were sold after the 1967 summer season, with three finding further service elsewhere in the BET group at Mexborough & Swinton.** *Martin Llewellyn*

The Duple group's 1962 range, availability and body prices:

Model	Built at	Chassis	Body price
Super Vega	Hendon	Bedford SB	£2,955
Gannet	Blackpool	Bedford SB, Thames	£2,955
Seagull 62	Blackpool	Bedford SB	£2,910
Seagull 62	Blackpool	Thames	£2,920
Bella Vista	Hendon	Bedford VAS	£2,585
Yeoman	Hendon	Thames	£2,955
Continental	Blackpool	Mid-engined	£3,650
Britannia front-entrance	Hendon	Mid-engined	£3,195
Britannia centre-entrance	Hendon	Mid-engined	£3,195
Donington	Loughborough	Mid-engined	£3,250
Seagull 70	Blackpool	Mid-engined	£3,250
Willowbrook Viscount	Loughborough	Mid-engined	£3,250

The rather plain Willowbrook Viscount looked distinctly over-priced when compared with the more attractive Seagull 70 and Britannia models.

Hendon-designed models would soon instil a new sense of order.

These new models started with the launch of the Bella Vista in the autumn of 1961 for the 1962 season. This neat design broke with Duple's curvaceous Vega and Vista tradition by having an almost straight waistline and much deeper areas of glazing than on any previous model. The whole styling ethos was squarer, and the Bella Vista was a considerable step forward from the models which had gone before. Gone, for example, were the drop-down opening side windows and in their place top-sliding vents were fitted as standard – they had been an option on the previous generation of Duple coaches.

The Bella Vista was a 29-seat body for fitment to the Bedford VAS. It was particularly favoured by Scottish operators running Highland tours and was to be found in the fleets of a number of Scottish Omnibuses Group subsidiaries. The biggest single order for the VAS/Bella Vista came from Scottish Omnibuses which took 20 in 1962, with 24 generously-spaced seats. The Bella Vista was also widely used in MacBrayne's touring fleet. It was just 23ft 9in long and 7ft 6in wide, making it ideal for touring in the far north of Scotland where many of the roads to the north and west of the Caledonian Canal still featured lengthy single track sections with passing places.

The Bella Vista was, as it transpired, just the beginning. It was followed in 1962 – for 1963 delivery – by the full-size Bella Vega for the best-selling Bedford SB chassis and by the identical Trooper for the Thames Trader. This body style for front-engined chassis was not engineered for either the Commer Avenger or the Albion Victor. For mid-engined chassis – the AEC Reliance and Leyland Leopard – a new 32ft-long Bella-style body was introduced, known as the Commodore. The original range of bodies featured a side flair towards the rear – this was known as the M-type moulding scheme – which was available with a polished insert at extra cost. The Commodore was short-lived, lasting for two seasons. In 1964 it would be joined – and then replaced – by the Commander, lacking the distinctive reverse-rake pillar towards the rear of the body which was a feature of the original Bella Vista, Bella Vega and Commodore models. The Commander was offered in two lengths – 32ft and 36ft.

These new bodies spelled the end for the Super Vega, Yeoman, Seagull 62, Seagull 70, Britannia, Gannet and Donington. The only bodies in 1963 which were not part of the Bella family were the two 11m models for mid-engined chassis, the Continental and limited-production Dragonfly, plus the new Firefly. A few of the last Britannias, in 1962, were built to a length of just over 31ft to accommodate 43 seats. The grille arrangement was altered towards the end of production, with the destination screen moved from below the windscreen to the bottom of the grille. Around the same time a single-piece windscreen was offered on forward-entrance models and a three-piece screen on centre-entrance coaches, as used on the 1962 bodies for front-engined chassis.

For operators requiring a smaller coach than the VAS, Bedford was offering the J2 goods vehicle chassis and a small number were fitted with rather plain coach bodies by Willowbrook. In 1963 Duple looked at the possibility of building a scaled-down Bella Vista which would have been an 18ft 10in long 19/20 seater. But J2 volumes were low, and production was left with Willowbrook; the body was later marketed and badged as the Duple Compact. Plaxton offered its altogether more stylish Consort body on the J2. The Consort was a diminutive Embassy.

Marshall of Cambridge took a brief look at the coach market in 1962, producing a body on a Thames Trader which was sold to local operator Miller Bros. It remained unique.

This was an exciting period in coach design, and Harrington joined the fray with a new Crusader III body for Ford and Bedford chassis in 1962. This looked much more like the Cavalier, and had the wrap-round windscreens adopted for the Crusader II in 1960 and fewer, longer, side windows. The Crusader III was also advertised as being available on the Albion Victor chassis, but none were built.

COMMANDER

by
DUPLE

41/51 passenger
Luxury Touring
Coach bodies for
A.E.C. or Leyland
U/F chassis

DUPLE GROUP SALES Ltd. EDGWARE RD., THE HYDE, LONDON N.W.9
FOR BODYWORK BY
DUPLE — WILLOWBROOK

TEL:- COLINDALE 6412

BLACKPOOL 62251

Left **The final version of Harrington's Crusader body on a Bedford SB in the fleet of Grey-Green Coaches. The deep side windows with their thin pillars were in keeping with the spirit of the time but the overall design was perhaps marred by the prominent and not very subtle front grille. The grille and the use of a straight waist reflect the style of the Legionnaire body for 36ft-long front-engined chassis. The location is Colchester bus station in the summer of 1966.** *Geoff Mills*

One final Crusader would appear, in 1964. This retained the windscreens of the previous model, but the remainder of the body was new with a straight waist, narrow pillars and – to reduce cost – composite construction. The previous Crusaders had been all-metal. Buyers of the Crusader IV included George Ewer and Thames Valley, but few were built.

There was some limited demand for double-deck coaches on busy services and in 1962 Ribble took delivery of 20 new White Ladies. These were Atlanteans with 59-seat Weymann bodies and they replaced the previous generation of distinctive fully-fronted Leyland Titan PD2s on busy express services in the North West. They lacked the polished mouldings of the Gay Hostesses which made them look just a bit utilitarian, relying on Ribble's cream coach livery to distinguish them externally from similar Atlantean buses. Crosville, too, used double-deck coaches on some of its services. Five Bristol Lodekka FLF6B coaches joined the Crosville fleet in 1962, followed by five more in 1964. These were 55-seaters with a luggage compartment at the rear of the lower deck and they were in the company's cream and black coach colours, rather than the standard Tilling green used for buses. They were used on express services linking Liverpool and North Wales.

One small operator who bought an Atlantean coach at this time was Silver Star of Porton Down. This had a lowbridge 61-seat Weymann body and was used on the company's express services which catered primarily for army personnel based on Salisbury Plain. Silver Star's coaches were distinguished by an illuminated panel on the front dome incorporating a star motif. The company was taken over by Wilts & Dorset in 1963.

Bedford was not going to be left out of the market for high-capacity 11m coaches, and in September 1962 it came up with an unconventional solution which maximised its commitment to using existing high-volume (and therefore low cost) truck componentry – the twin-steer Bedford VAL. This featured a vertical front-mounted engine, the 131bhp Leyland O.400. A Turner five-speed gearbox was fitted, and a two-speed rear axle was available. The two front axles were set back, allowing a front entrance ahead of the wheels. These were small, 16in diameter (the same as on the diminutive

Left centre **An early Bedford VAL with Duple Vega Major body pauses in Auchterarder in the summer of 1963. The operator was Watson of Dundee, a 12-vehicle coach business. Duple exercised considerable skill in using the same basic design treatment for coaches seating 29, 41 and 52 people.** *Iain MacGregor*

Left below **The long and the short of it. Plaxton's Panorama body on the three-axle Bedford was**

simply styled Val. A Val operated by Price's Coaches of Halesowen poses alongside Plaxton's diminutive Consort, based on a modified Bedford J2 goods chassis. The Consort was owned by Wheatley of Patricroft. Note how the same basic grille treatment is successfully applied to two quite different vehicles. Both Bedfords were entrants in the 1963 Blackpool coach rally. A Duple-bodied Thames stands in the background. *Michael Fowler*

Below **Plaxton's stand at the 1962 Earl's Court show. On the left is a Reliance with Panorama bodywork for Sheffield United, while on the right is the first Bedford VAL to be fitted with Plaxton body, for Bloomfields Coaches of London. It has eight main side windows, which was a feature of a small number of early Plaxton bodies on 36ft-long chassis. The wide-angle lens makes the VAL look squatter than it actually was.** *Plaxton*

VAS), compared with the industry standard of 20in. The VAL ran on 8.25x16 tyres. This gave a floor height of just over 3ft, compared with around 3ft 6in on a mid-engined Leopard or Reliance. To ease potential problems with heavy steering on a coach with four steered wheels, Bedford fitted power-assisted steering as standard. The twin-steer layout gave a high-quality ride, and Bedford also promoted it as a safety feature, including a demonstration in which a blow-out at speed was induced in one of the front tyres to show that this did not seriously affect the coach's directional stability.

The VAL was also notably less expensive than the 36ft-long models from AEC and Leyland, with a list price of £1,775, which was roughly £1,000 less than the heavyweights. Bodywork for the VAL initially came from Duple with the Vega Major (in effect a stretched Bella Vega), and from Plaxton with a variant of the Panorama which was badged quite simply Val,

although the first VAL to be bodied, for Bloomfields Coaches of London, had a lengthened multi-windowed Embassy II, which was destined to be unique. The VAL chassis had a front-mounted radiator, and Plaxton's bodies on early VALs used the large oval grille which was carried over from the Embassy body fitted to the front-engined SB and Thames. Eleven VALs were bodied by Yeates, including six which had two doors for Barton Transport.

Where Duple, Plaxton and Yeates effectively offered stretched versions of existing bodies on the VAL, Harrington came up with something completely new: the Legionnaire. This bore no resemblance to the stylish Cavalier and Grenadier and was angular – almost utilitarian – in its appearance. True, it had long deep side windows in the fashion of the times, but without the panache of those bodies offered by Duple and Plaxton. Launched in 1963, it was reworked in 1964 with a change to the roof profile intro-

ducing an element of curvature. At the same time fixed windows and forced-air ventilation were made standard features. Only 42 VALs were bodied by Harrington including vehicles for such well-known companies as Barton Transport (eight), Epsom Coaches (five), Yelloway (four) and the George Ewer group (two).

Bodied VALs weighed around 6 tons 10 cwt, at a time when a 36ft-long Reliance or Leopard coach typically weighed between 7 tons 10 cwt and 8 tons. The VAL's gross vehicle weight was 11 tons 10cwt – one ton less than a 36ft Leopard or Reliance. In a 1963 road test by the weekly newspaper *Motor Transport*, a Duple-bodied VAL gave an average fuel consumption figure of 15.88mpg (which compared with 16.3mpg for a Bedford SB tested by the same journal in 1962).

As with most Bedford coaches, the VAL was favoured by small operators. The first in

Plaxton Embassy II 51-52 seater
on Bedford VAL chassis

increase of one third. Other changes were made to the braking system at the same time. The handbrake operated on the two front axles and was backed up by a drum-type transmission brake, as fitted to the VAS.

The VAL was a success, giving small operators an affordable high-capacity coach which promised lower running costs than the heavyweight models from AEC and Leyland. Sales in 1963 reached almost 200, and in 1965 were not far short of 300. No other 36ft coach was selling in anything like those numbers to independent fleets, with long Reliances and Leopards only achieving double figure sales to small operators.

Overshadowed by the launch of the VAL was an upgrade of the SB range with the introduction of the more powerful SB5, which took over from the SB3. The "5" indicated the fitment of Bedford's 330 cu in (5.42 litre) diesel which provided 105bhp. Bedford was also offering Leyland engines – initially the 105bhp O.350 in the SB8 from 1957, and then the 115bhp O.370 in the SB13 from 1963. Leyland-engined Bedfords were often favoured by bigger fleets – Tilling companies Eastern National, South Midland and London-based Tillings Transport all ran SBs with Leyland engines, as did Southern Vectis which had been buying Bedfords for touring on the Isle of Wight since 1939. Southern Vectis had a dozen SB8s and five SB13s, all bodied by Duple. Three Thames Valley SB13s delivered in 1964 were unusual in having Harrington bodies, the first for a Tilling company since 1950.

While Plaxton facelifts were less frequent than those of Duple, there were a few and the most notable in the early 1960s was the short-lived Embassy III for Thames Trader and Bedford SB chassis. This dispensed with the peaked dome of the Embassy II and featured a one-piece windscreen and a straight waist. In general outline it foreshadowed a restyle coming in 1965 but with a strange ribbed grille flanked by pairs of twin vertical headlights. The Embassy III was launched at the 1963 Scottish Motor Show and lasted just one season.

Having seen Ford successfully win a share of the lightweight coach business with its Thames Trader psv chassis, Dodge decided to have a go and in 1962 announced the S307 which was offered with a choice of front-mounted vertical

Scotland went to Park of Hamilton in the spring of 1963 – a 52-seat Plaxton-bodied coach in Park's distinctive all-over black livery. Scotland's biggest user was Edinburgh City Transport. It bought six in 1964 to replace some of its Royal Tigers, and by 1970 had 15. Other early fleet buyers included West Riding which had three, although they only lasted two years, and Barton Transport which bought 20 in 1963-64 with bodies by all four of the coachbuilders then bodying VALs – Duple, Harrington, Plaxton and Yeates. The first VALs

for a Tilling company went to Southern Vectis in 1964 – ultimately there would be 12 in the fleet.

Brake performance and lining wear proved to be a source of concern on the VAL, something which Bedford may have anticipated as it offered the option of an exhaust brake. In 1965 the width of the front and rear linings was increased, upping the lining area per ton of gross weight from 47.6sq in to 63sq in – an

Right **The Embassy III from Plaxton featured twin headlights set in vertical pairs. Grille apart, the straight waist and big windows gave a foretaste of the direction in which the Embassy body was heading. This 1964 Bedford SB5 had been new to Wingrove of Hazlemere but later headed north to operate for Carruthers of New Abbey.**
Trevor Brookes

Below **Rickards of London alighted on this unlikely combination in 1964 – a Dodge with a Strachan body. Dodge was trying, without success, to break into the bus and coach business with a front-engined chassis which had a set-back front axle. In this it beat both Bedford and Ford into production with a layout which would prove popular with small operators for the following 20 years. Rickards bought six, and Strachan built the bodies, which looked good for the company's first attempt at a modern coach. This one is at Heathrow in British Eagle colours. Rickards livery was maroon.**
Maurice Bateman

engines – the Leyland O.370 or the Perkins 6.354. Where it scored over the existing models from Bedford and Ford was in the provision of a set-back front axle, which allowed the entrance to be positioned in the front overhang. Coach operators remained unimpressed. The only Dodge coaches built were six with Perkins engines for Rickards of Brentford in 1964. They had steel-framed Strachan Pacemaker bodies.

Strachan, based in Hamble, was developing a Pacemaker II coach for mid-engined chassis, but none were built. The company's last major involvement in coaching was the supply of what were in reality 26 dual-purpose bodies on Ford R-series chassis to Evan Evans Tours of London in 1968. A small number of similar coaches were supplied to other fleets at the same time.

Ford also tackled the small coach market in which Bedford was establishing an effective monopoly with the VAS. Ford's offering was the Thames FC chassis, with bodywork by Kenex Coachwork of Dover who were primarily builders of utilitarian works buses. For the Thames FC, Kenex came up with a stylish 25 or 29 seat body with a three-piece wrap-round windscreen resembling that fitted to the Duple Yeoman. The Thames 534E, based on an existing 3-ton Trader truck chassis, was available in two wheelbases for bodies of 22ft 1in or 23ft 11in overall length, and was powered by a choice of a four-cylinder 3.61-litre diesel or, in

the 532E, 3.26-litre petrol engine. Although competitively priced at £3,137 for the 29-seater, the Kenex-bodied Thames never really matched the Bedford VAS/Duple in terms of sales. The model had its first showing at the 1962 British Coach Rally when one was entered by Whitefriars Coaches of London. In September 1962 Kenex was taken over by Martin Walter of Folkestone and the body was christened the Romney by its new owners – but it soon disappeared, unable to compete with the popular Bedford VAS/Duple Bella Vista.

Also offering bodywork on the small Thames (and on the Bedford VAS) was Thurgood of Ware. This was the Forerunner (on the Thames) and the Successor (on the Bedford), a competently-styled low-volume model, selling for £3,250 on the VAS in 1964. Thurgood withdrew from bodybuilding in 1967, its premises being taken over by Plaxton as a southern service centre. Portsmouth-based Reading built on the VAS too, but like other small builders could not compete with the all-conquering Bella Vista. An old-fashioned body with shallow windows supplied to Enterprise Coaches of Leicester in 1964 was among Reading's last.

While there had been some considerable rebuilding and rebodying of coaches in the early 1950s, there was little in the 1960s, except where accident damage made it worthwhile to fit a new body to an existing chassis. The major

A few builders tried to break in to the market for coaches of 29 seats or fewer, but none really challenged the success of Bedford. Ford produced a short Thames Trader model which was bodied by Kenex, who were taken over by Martin Walter. Few were built by either manufacturer. Thurgood also bodied the small Thames – but neither of the two major players, Duple and Plaxton, got involved with it. Shearings – in 1963 a relatively little-known name – operated this Martin Walter Romney.
Michael Fowler

exception to this was a batch of Midland Red C3 coaches which had BMMO-built mid-engined chassis and centre-entrance Willowbrook bodies which with their curvaceous lines were looking just a bit dated at the start of the 1960s. The decision was taken to scrap the old bodies on 16 chassis and to have them rebodied in 1963 by Plaxton with 36-seat Panorama bodies. The rear overhang was extended to make the rebuilt coaches 31ft 8in long, and to suit the chassis' front-mounted radiators the bodies used the large oval Embassy-style grille. One more C3 was rebodied in 1964 and all 17 coaches ran for a further seven years. The rebodied coaches, classified CL3 by Midland Red, originally oper-

Right A Bedford VAS1 with Thurgood Successor body for Elms Coaches of Kenton. This 1967 coach was Thurgood's last, although the company's Ware site found continued use as a southern service centre for Plaxton. The body has overtones of Duple styles of earlier in the decade in the side mouldings and the grille. *Geoff Mills*

Below Yeates produced bodies which were a bit different from those coming out of the mainstream coach builders. This Europa from the fleet of Wilson of Failsworth, near Bolton, illustrates the unusua – for 1960 – paint schemes used by Yeates and the bold frontal appearance. The little tail fins were an unusual styling feature. Beneath the jazzy paint the basic body shape was quite pleasing. Most Europas were built on Bedford chassis; this one is unusual in being on a Thames. An earlier style of Yeates body from the same operator stands behind. *Capital Transport*

Left above Still unmistakably a Yeates product, but now with a more restrained front end, this is a 1963 Fiesta FE44 operated by Premier of Stainforth. The Fiesta FE44 used a modified Bedford SB chassis which allowed the entrance to be located in the front overhang. The concept had been pioneered by Yeates in 1960 with the Pegasus – the Pegasus had vertical window pillars while the Fiesta had sloping pillars and bigger windows. *Michael Fowler*

Left below The first 36ft-long bodies from Yeates were six Europas on AEC Reliance chassis in 1962 for Barton Transport. These were unusual in having two doors. They were followed in 1963 by seven two-door VALs. Barton operated a Glasgow to Corby express service, introduced to serve relocated steel workers. A Reliance is seen in Glasgow in the autumn of 1962. It carries the Robin Hood name on the front, following Barton's takeover of that company in 1961. *Iain MacGregor*

Right above When this stylish Alexander-bodied coach was unveiled at the 1961 Scottish Motor Show in Glasgow's Kelvin Hall, no one would have dared predict a production run spanning two decades for the new Y-type body. The first coach, on a 36ft Reliance, was built for use on the Edinburgh to London service of Scottish Omnibuses. Production bodies used a grille with a finer mesh. The coach is seen in 1964 after being repainted in the darker green livery adopted by Scottish Omnibuses in that year. The coach on the right shows the previous lighter green. *Stewart J Brown*

Right A few operators took Y-type coaches without the roof-mounted destination display which was a feature of production bodies. These included Hebble, with this one-off delivery in 1966 on a 36ft-long Reliance. Non-standard beading has been applied to accommodate Hebble's livery layout. The illuminated side panel for the fleetname was an option on the Y-type. This coach is at Lichfield heading to Cheltenham on the South West Clipper service, which was run as part of the Associated Motorways network and which also involved the independent Wallace Arnold company. *Martin Llewellyn*

ated in overall cream but were soon repainted red. Midland Red's CL3 rebodying programme followed the fitment in 1962 of new 26-seat Plaxton Embassy-style bodies to three 12-year-old C2-class coaches.

Having taken over Burlingham in 1960 Duple expanded further in 1963 when it bought the Loughborough body shop of W S Yeates. Yeates had been building coach bodies since 1946. Output in 1959 was around 70, but by 1962 was down to under 50. The vast majority of Yeates bodies were built on front-engined chassis and were distinguished by flamboyant paint schemes which helped conceal rather staid, but not unattractive, styling – apart, perhaps, from the garish grilles on some later models. The Europa was built from 1956 to 1963, and was joined in 1960 by the Fiesta, which featured sloping window pillars.

The most novel product to come from Yeates was the Pegasus, launched in 1960. The Pegasus was built on a modified Bedford SB chassis, on which the front axle was relocated rearwards by some 18 inches, giving space for an entrance ahead of the front wheel and thus anticipating Bedford's VAM range of 1965. Most Pegasuses were in fact dual-purpose vehicles, rather than pure coaches, but when the Fiesta FE44 was added to the range in 1962, using a similarly modified Bedford SB chassis, it was specified as a 44-seat coach by a number of operators. Eighteen were built. The last Yeates coach body was a Fiesta on a Bedford VAL for Rickards of Brentford. Although it sold its body shop to Duple, Yeates retained its coach dealing activities in Loughborough.

Left The original style of MCW Topaz body on a pre-production Bedford VAL chassis proved to be a one-off. It is seen here at the 1962 Commercial Motor Show before a short spell as a demonstrator. The body was transferred to a production VAL and entered service with Rowson of Hayes in 1963. *Stephen Barber collection*

Below The Topaz II of 1965 bore no resemblance to the original body of the same name. It had bigger windows, and more coach-like side mouldings. Clarke's of London SE20 was one of just six buyers to take a Topaz II body on a VAL. The company's rare coach still looks smart at Gilwell Park Scout Jamboree in 1971 flanked by a Plaxton Embassy II and an elderly Duple Super Vega. *Trevor Brookes*

In Scotland, a new body from Alexander was to have a profound impact on both coach and bus operation for the following three decades. This was the Y-type. The first Y-type, in 1961, was an unusual three-door Leopard bus for Edinburgh City Transport, a vehicle whose layout was such a talking point that few realised the far-reaching influence which the new Alexander body would have.

The vehicle which demonstrated the Y-type's potential was a 36ft AEC Reliance for Scottish Omnibuses. This, the first of a new generation of London service coaches, had the big fixed trapezoidal windows which would become a hallmark of the Y-type and it featured forced-air ventilation for the first time in a Scottish Omnibuses Group coach. It differed from production models in detail, most notably an unusual circular window at the rear where the toilet was located, and the fitment of twin destination screens below the windscreen. But the basic concept was there for all to see, and it was one of the great success stories of the time.

Forced-air ventilation was still something of a novelty in the early 1960s, and as people grappled with the concept some odd descriptions were coined. *Commercial Motor*, not renowned for its use of words derived from Hindi, described the Y-type as having "ventilation by punkah louvre", a description no doubt as mystifying then as it is now. The *New Collins Concise English Dictionary* comes to the rescue with the definition: "a large fan made of palm leaves etc, worked mechanically to cool a room".

Forced-air ventilation was not always very satisfactory. On many designs it depended on the driver remembering to switch on the fans, without which the jet-vents above the passengers were ineffective. A few operators toyed with the fitment of full air-conditioning and there were two air-conditioned coaches at the 1963 British Coach Rally – a Plaxton-bodied Reliance owned by Sheffield United, and a rather unlikely vehicle in the shape of a Duple-bodied Bedford SB5 owned by Hastings Coachways. This had been a Duple Motor Show exhibit and was bought for use on tours to Greece, something of a marathon trip for a lightweight coach. In the event the SB5 proved to be a shade under-powered because of the

MCW **TOPAZ** II

power drawn by the air-conditioning

But back to the Y-type. Coaches with Y-type bodies with reclining seats and toilets were soon running to London from Edinburgh and Glasgow, setting new standards of comfort and style. The early London coaches were built on Reliance chassis with AH470 engines for Scottish Omnibuses and on Leopard PSU3/3s for Western SMT. The adaptable Y-type was also built as a touring coach and, in true Scottish group fashion, as a dual-purpose vehicle with jack-knife doors in place of the single-piece slam door of the original coaches. It was as a dual-purpose coach that the Y-type would make its mark in Scotland.

Alexander were bus builders and their success in coach manufacture was largely down to the company's close relationship with the Scottish Omnibuses Group and a growing number of BET fleets. Early BET users of the Y-type were Hebble (two Reliances, 1964), North Western (10 Leopards in 1964, followed by 10 more in 1965) and Trent (eight Leopards, 1964). The only independents to buy Y-type coaches were Premier Travel of Cambridge, Venture Transport of Consett, Hutchison of Overtown (two in 1967) and the Glasgow-based Scottish Co-operative Wholesale Society, trading as Majestic, which took five. Premier Travel's Y-types were used primarily on express services while Venture's were really dual-purpose vehicles for use on stage services. Those supplied to SCWS, on AEC Reliance chassis, were genuine coaches and were unusual in hav-

ing a plain front dome and destination displays below the windscreen as on the original Scottish Omnibuses prototype. The only other buyers of production Y-types with plain front domes were Central SMT (on Albion Vikings), Highland Omnibuses (on Bedford VAMs) and Hebble (on AEC Reliances).

MCW were also bus builders and despite the limited success of the Fanfare, still had the idea that there was a place for the company in coaching. For the Bedford VAL it produced the ungainly multi-windowed Topaz, which was in the demonstration park at the 1962 Commercial Motor Show, the year in which Fanfare production finally petered out. Only one was built. It was operated by Rowson of Hayes, although not on the pre-production chassis to which it was originally fitted. The original Topaz metamorphosed into the rather more attractive, but still slightly odd, Topaz II in 1965. Like the Fanfare and its derivatives, the Topaz was an all-metal structure and with the launch of the Topaz II MCW were hopeful of great things. Not only did it have "classic lines, 20th century comfort and a great future" (to quote MCW's sales brochure), it claimed to be the lightest 36ft coach on Britain's roads, with an unladen weight of just 5 tons 15 cwt. This, said MCW, meant fuel consumption of 17.6mpg – a figure which it does seems hard to credit. MCW offered the Topaz II on other 36ft chassis – more of which anon.

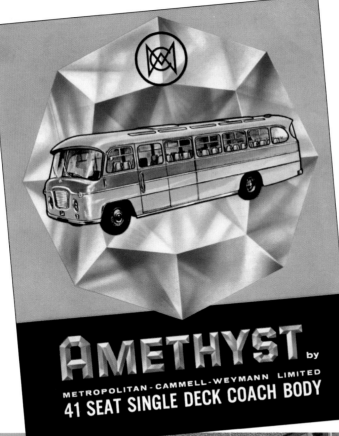

Right **One of the flops of the 1960s – MCW's Amethyst, for which no-one placed any orders. A single example was built for the 1962 Commercial Motor Show.**

Below **In 1961 ECW introduced a new coach body for the Bristol MW chassis. This had a stepped waistline and was a much more convincing coach than the model which it replaced. The first, for Tillings Transport, had an oval grille which was not used on production bodies. This former Tillings coach is seen running for Eastern National in 1970 – there was considerable movement of vehicles between the two companies in the 1960s.** *Iain MacGregor*

The 52-seat Topaz II body had a list price of £3,650 when mounted on a Bedford VAL chassis, compared to £3,920 for Duple's Vega Major body. But Duple had a proven track record, an established dealer network and good second-hand values – none of which could be said about MCW, at least in relation to its coaches. Which is why even with a 10 per cent price advantage the Topaz II didn't take the world by storm and MCW's London office switchboard at Tate Gallery 7777 (no kidding!) was not being swamped by eager coach operators. Only six Bedford VALs were fitted with Topaz II bodies. They were bought by Wallace Arnold, Jones of Aberbeeg, Clarke's of London SE20, Billie's of Mexborough, Fox of Hayes and Davies of Tredegar.

A companion to the original Topaz, and equally unsuccessful, was the Amethyst,

Right **The ECW coach body for the Bristol MW went through a number of detail changes. It was lengthened slightly – the added length being incorporated in the rearmost side window, and it was given deeper windscreens. A new style of grille was adopted, based loosely on the outline of the traditional Bristol radiator. These changes are incorporated on this 1964 coach operated by Hants & Dorset. The last batch of bodies, in 1966, would have a straight waist, with equal depth windows front to rear.** *W T Lambden*

for the Bedford SB. It was announced in 1962 and was on display at that year's Earls Court show. Only one was built, this despite the best efforts of MCW's brochure copy-writer who, in extolling the Amethyst's virtues, pointed out "There is even a receptacle for litter at the end of the best possible journey" and added, somewhat enigmatically "Equipment is comprehensive – extras really are extras". Well, that's reassuring. Both the Topaz and the Amethyst were built in the Weymann factory at Addlestone. Neither proved to be the gems which their names implied.

The relaxation of the length limits brought a new model from Bristol. Its MW, the mid-engined 30ft chassis, remained in production unaltered, although ECW produced a more attractive coach body which took advantage of the relaxed limits to incorporate a nicely styled front and rear, taking what was nominally a 30ft coach to a length of around 31ft. A prototype entered service with Tillings in 1961 and production got under way in 1962.

But for 36ft operation Bristol opted for a new rear-engined chassis, the RE, powered by a horizontal Gardner engine. It was introduced in 1962. For this ECW built an express coach body which was similar in concept to the new body on the MW, but with long side windows. The prototype had a stepped waist rail, but this was not adopted for production bodies. An unusual feature was the use of a Lodekka-style grille on the front of the body to provide a flow of air to the RE's front-mounted radiator. At this early stage in the RE's life all sales were to Tilling group companies. Early buyers of the RE coach included United Auto, Bristol Omnibus and Royal Blue, all for express services running into London. The rear-mounted engine meant low noise levels throughout most of the interior.

The Bristol Omnibus REs arrived as the company was strengthening its coaching identity using the Bristol Greyhound brand name. Greyhound Motors had in 1925 been a pioneering express coach operator running from Bristol to London. It had been taken over by Bristol Tramways (the predecessor of Bristol Omnibus) in 1928, but a Greyhound logo had been used on many of the Bristol company's coaches down the years. In 1960 the Bristol Greyhound name had been adopted, along with a cream and maroon livery, in place of cream and green. The maroon was changed to red in 1963.

The RE was the first mass-production rear-engined psv chassis in Britain (although the lay-out was already in widespread use in the USA and in Europe) and it got off to a flying start. By the end of 1964 there were 119 RE coaches in service with Tilling companies. It was also the most successful, enjoying a long production run and suffering few of the problems of reliability and durability which would plague most of its rear-engined contemporaries.

A rather different rear-engined coach was exhibited at the 1962 Commercial Motor Show,

Above **For the 36ft-long Bristol RE ECW produced a body which had clearly been designed by the same hand as had developed the MW body. The RE body had longer fixed windows, and used a Lodekka-style grille. A Bristol Greyhound coach pauses in Marlborough on its way from London to Bristol in the days when the A4 was the main route.** *Martin Llewellyn*

In 1964 United Automobile Services put 20 Bristol RELH6Gs into service. They had ECW bodies with 45 seats, offering reasonably generous legroom for long-distance travellers. They were regular performers on the Newcastle to London service and this one is seen in Leicester. United's bodies had non-standard side mouldings and, although the coaches were bought for long-distance operation, specified the optional two-piece express-type door. *Chris Aston*

as Mercedes-Benz made the first of what would be a number of attempts to sell coaches in the UK. It exhibited a left-hand-drive O.321HL integral with a 5.1-litre 110bhp engine and a selling price of £6,500. A 126bhp 5.6-litre engine was an extra-cost option. None were sold.

It was 1964 before further rear-engined models would appear, and in the meantime Ford entered the market for 36ft coaches with the Thames 36, announced in 1963. This, chassis type 676E, had a front-mounted engine (the same as on the existing Trader 570E) but, unlike its three-axle rival from Bedford, used normal-sized wheels and tyres. A Clarke five-speed gearbox and Eaton two-speed rear axle were standard features. A set-back front axle allowed the provision of front-entrance bodywork, giving almost the same ease of access as was offered on coaches based on more expensive underfloor-engined chassis. However the engine did protrude above floor level (as did that on the Bedford VAL) which meant access wasn't as good as on a Leopard or Reliance, and internal noise levels were higher too.

For the Thames 36 Duple produced the 52-seat Marauder body which was generally similar to the Vega Major on the Bedford VAL, but was five inches taller because of the higher chassis frame on the Thames. A detail difference on the Marauder was the absence of the side flair thanks to a new, simplified pattern of body mouldings, known by Duple as the N-type scheme and soon applied across the range. Bodywork for the Thames 36 was also available from Plaxton and Harrington, the latter building the angular Legionnaire as fitted to the Bedford VAL. Harrington-bodied Thames 36s were few in number, with production barely reaching double figures.

An eye-catching variant of Duple's Bella family was announced for the 1964 season – the Astrocoach. This was in effect a Commander with glazed cove panels and a thin cantrail to create the impression of continuous glazing from the waistrail into the roof. Only one was built, on an AEC Reliance which was sold to Smiths of Wigan. It had low-backed seats, no doubt to add to the feeling of spaciousness, but only lasted a very short time with Smiths before being sold to Monks of Leigh. Duple's drawing office produced plans for a short 26ft version of the Astrocoach which would have been called the Isabella. On a non-standard AEC Reliance with a shortened wheelbase of just 13ft 7in, the 35-seat Isabella – which would also have been 7ft 6in wide – never got off the drawing board.

While the steadily-growing motorway network offered clear benefits for long-distance travel, it could also help speed-up shorter journeys. In the autumn of 1964 London Transport took advantage of the M1 to introduce an hourly service from Victoria to Tring using the motorway. The effect of what might have been viewed as the dawn of a new era for Green Line operation was perhaps undermined by the use of 10-year-old RF-type Regal IVs on the new 727

Harrington

Legionnaire

52 seater

36ft x 8ft 2½ins coach body

for

Bedford VAL chassis and Ford Thames 36ft chassis

Duple built just one Astrocoach, based on the Commander body but with glazed cove panels which were separated from the main side windows by just a narrow strip. It was initially operated by Smiths of Wigan, but was later bought by Rennie of Dunfermline in whose ownership it is seen at the 1969 Dunoon Highland Games. The cover of Duple's Astrocoach brochure is shown below.
Iain MacGregor

service. However in the following year some slightly more coach-like vehicles did join the Green Line fleet with the arrival of 14 AEC Reliance 690s, the RC class. These had air suspension (which soon proved troublesome), five-speed automatic gearboxes, and 49 high-backed seats in a BET-style Willowbrook body. They wore a new livery of pale grey with a band of green relief, and were allocated to the 705 running from Windsor to Sevenoaks.

The BET style body – also built by Marshall and Weymann – was at times completed to quite a high specification for express services. In this guise it was favoured by some of BET's Yorkshire subsidiaries and by a few independents, such as MacBrayne.

Midland Red took advantage of the 1961 relaxation in vehicle lengths to develop a lengthened version of its CM5 motorway coach. This, the CM6, appeared in prototype form in 1963, and in production form in 1965-66 when 29 were built. The prototype used the same windows as the CM5, but production coaches

GENERAL SPECIFICATION

71

Below **A drawing showing the Isabella, conceived by Duple as a short-length 35-seat Astrocoach. None were built.**

Bottom **Red House of Coventry supported its local chassis manufacturer by buying a Roadliner in 1967. It had a Plaxton Panorama I body. Note the small grille below the last window to provide ventilation for the engine bay. The string of names along the side are operators which became part of the Red House group. The absence of wheel trims at a time when they were *de rigeur* for independents' coaches gives the Roadliner a slightly uncared for look.** *Trevor Brookes*

Right **The Park Royal-bodied Albion Viking was a crisply-styled coach – and a flop. The fluted side mouldings at skirt level were impractical, being vulnerable to damage and more expensive to repair than a simple steel or aluminium panel. But more importantly, neither Albion nor Park Royal had any standing in the coach market. Only six were built. One was purchased by Hirst of Holmfirth.** *Geoff Lumb*

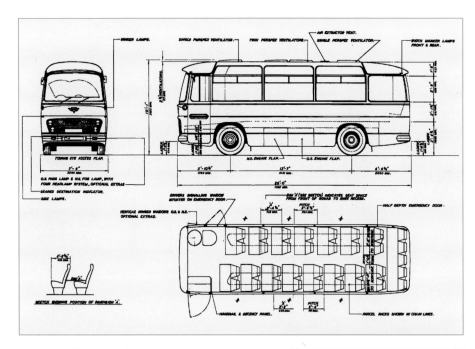

had longer bays and a simplified windscreen and grille. In place of the cove-mounted route boards of the CM5, the CM6s had illuminated cove panels above the four main side windows which read, for example, London Birmingham Motorway Express.

Mechanically, the CM6 had a bigger engine – still BMMO-built, but of 10.5-litre capacity. The CM6 also had a semi-automatic gearbox. The CM6s lasted until the mid-1970s, covering high mileages on motorway express services – some by then in National white livery.

Leyland updated its 30ft L-series Leopards in 1964, incorporating PSU3 parts – such as the heavier-duty front axle – and recoding the coach chassis as the PSU4/3 with manual gearbox and the PSU4/4 with the semi-automatic Pneumocyclic. Air suspension remained an option, while coach operators remained suspicious. Most Leopards were built with conventional steel springs. Fewer than 100 L-series Leopards had been sold as coaches to independents, and annual sales of the PSU4 to small coach operators were generally in single figures – partly because if an operator was going to invest in a heavyweight coach it might as well be a maximum-length 36ft one, rather than a 30ft vehicle with its lower carrying capacity. Only around 75 PSU4 coaches were sold to independents over a 15-year production life – and that figure included 30 for Wallace Arnold.

Four rear-engined chassis were announced in 1964 – the Daimler Roadliner, AEC Swift, Leyland Panther and Leyland Panther Cub. Leyland had taken over AEC in 1962, and the new models from both companies were intended primarily for urban bus operation, with low front frames to allow a single-step entrance. However an attempt was made to promote the Panther as a coach, with but limited success.

The PSUR1/2R Panther coach chassis differed from the PSUR1/1R bus in having a straight frame and Leyland's horizontal O.600 engine, initially rated at 130bhp (instead of 125bhp) for coach operation. The power output would be upped to 140bhp from 1968. The bigger O.680, rated at 150bhp, was also available. The Panther coach had longer front springs than the bus, and a Leyland Pneumocyclic gearbox was fitted as standard; there was no manual option. Coach operators were not queuing up to buy the Panther. The first coach, with BET-style dual-purpose body by Marshall of Cambridge,

was built for Ribble and was in the demonstration park at the 1964 Commercial Motor Show. It ran for Ribble until 1975. The only small operators to buy Panther coaches in the 1960s were Soudley Valley Coaches of Cinderford, Seamarks of Luton (which bravely took 16) and Skills of Nottingham, with two. All 19 had Plaxton bodies; no Panthers were bodied by Duple.

The Seamarks vehicles were christened Powercrusairs and had the optional air suspension which proved troublesome. Problems with 1960s air suspension systems included the air bags becoming dislocated, levelling valves failing (which upset the balance of the system) and fractures of the locating leaf spring. The Plaxton Panorama I bodies for Seamarks had additional fluted chrome trim at wheelarch level, intended to match the chrome around the waist area at the front of the body. Seamarks also specified curtains, which were rare at that time, and TV sets – among the first to be fitted to a British coach.

The Roadliner, too, was designed with the urban bus market in mind, but with its powerful Cummins V6 engine was – on paper at least –

ideally suited to long-distance motorway cruising. One of the first Roadliner demonstrators was a coach with Duple Commander body. The 9.6-litre Cummins engine was compact, fitting neatly under the rear seats, and it was rated at 150bhp, making the Roadliner the most powerful coach on the British market. The Roadliner had a Daimatic four-speed semi-automatic gearbox, with no manual option.

Daimler coaches were few and far between in 1964 – the odd 1950s Freeline and the occasional elderly CVD6. But Daimler had taken the bus market by storm with its Fleetline double-decker, and was no doubt hoping to do the same with the Roadliner in the coach market. Conservative independents – wisely, as it turned out – waited to see how it would shape up, but Black & White Motorways, understandably impressed by the Roadliner's specification, ordered eight with Cummins engines and Plaxton bodies which were delivered in 1966-67. PMT, which built up a fleet of Roadliner buses, also took three coaches with Plaxton bodies in 1967, followed by three Duple-bodied examples in 1968. The Roadliner was plagued with reliability problems almost from the outset,

and vibration from the Cummins V6 added to its troubles by affecting the bodies, with trim being shaken loose and falling off.

One more rear-engined chassis was to make an appearance. This was the high-framed Albion Viking VK43, introduced in 1965. The power plant was Leyland's 125bhp vertical O.400 engine, driving through an Albion constant mesh gearbox. The Viking had a 16ft 2in wheelbase and was designed for 32ft long bodywork – which meant a long linkage for the gear lever – and had been developed primarily to meet the operating requirements of the ever conservative Scottish Bus Group (as the Scottish Omnibuses Group was known from 1963). Most Vikings had Alexander Y-type bodies, including five fairly luxurious coaches for Central SMT – which were soon moved on to Highland Omnibuses, at that time a depository for vehicles which were not wanted by other SBG companies.

The vertical engine intruded into the body, which meant that despite a gain of 2ft in length SBG's Vikings seated only 40 people – one fewer than 1950s Tiger Cubs – with a large and not very practical luggage area behind the rear

73

seats. A demonstrator with Alexander Y-type body did the rounds, visiting BET fleets such as Aldershot & District and Hebble. But the Viking was not a particularly impressive vehicle. The steering was light, the gearchange was awkward, the engine was noisy, the overall layout poor and the demonstrator, not surprisingly, failed to win any business. The Viking was also more expensive than the mass-produced lightweight chassis with which it was most likely to be compared.

But in another brave attempt to sell into the lightweight coach market – after the failure of the Victor VT21L – Leyland commissioned industrial design consultants John and Sylvia Reid to come up with a body which Park Royal could build on the rear-engined Albion. The result was striking. The Park Royal Royalist (reviving a name used for a short-lived mid-1950s coach body) was crisp and modern, albeit still using ash and teak in the body framing, at a time when Park Royal's bus bodies were of all-metal construction. The Reids styled the interior as well as the exterior and the new coach was unveiled at the 1966 Commercial Motor Show, in the livery of Eatonways of Birmingham, who never actually operated it.

Park Royal promoted the Royalist as being suitable not only for the Viking, but also for the Bedford VAL and VAM, and Ford R192 and

R226. Had the Royalist been built by Duple and mounted on a Bedford chassis it would have been a winner. But Park Royal's track record in coaches wasn't good – matched only by the equally unimpressive performance of Albion. No coach operator was going to seriously invest in a Park Royal-bodied Albion and, rather sadly, only six were built. Four were sold to the Coventry-based Red House group; the other two were sold to Clyde Coast of Saltcoats and Hirst of Holmfirth after short spells on demonstration duties. This was Albion's last foray into the coach market.

The Bedford VAM and the Ford R192 and R226 were altogether more significant 1965 launches. These new models offered Bedford and Ford users the advantages of an entrance opposite the driver in the front overhang, and an extra four seats in a body which was around 32ft long. Four seats may not sound much, but think of it as a 10 per cent increase in carrying capacity and the attraction becomes obvious.

The VAM was launched as the VAM5 with the Bedford 330 engine as used in the SB and a four-speed gearbox. It had a wheelbase of 16ft 1in. Options included the choice of two five-speed gearboxes – one with overdrive top – and a two-speed rear axle. The Leyland O.400 which powered the VAL was available as an option in the VAM14, giving 131bhp instead of the more

modest 107bhp of Bedford's own engine. The five-speed overdrive gearbox came as standard with the more powerful engine, and VAM14s also had 24 volt electrics, rather than the 12 volt system used on Bedford-engined chassis. The VAM quickly replaced the SB in most operators' orders, but the older model continued in production for those needing a more compact coach. Scottish operator MacBrayne, for example, continued to buy SB coaches until 1970 and the SB continued to sell in low volumes right through the 1970s.

At Ford the launch of the new R-series models meant the death of the old 570E Trader and the dropping of the Thames name. Like the VAM, the R192 and the companion R226 (which replaced the Thames 36) had a vertical engine mounted in the front overhang. The standard engine in the shorter R192 was the 4.91-litre Ford 330 diesel rated at 115bhp, driving through a four-speed gearbox. The R226 used the bigger 5.95-litre 360 which delivered 128bhp, and was linked to a five-speed gearbox. This drive train was offered as an option on the R192. The old Thames 36 had a 100bhp engine.

The figure in the chassis code was the wheelbase in inches; the R192 was designed for 45-seat bodywork up to 32ft long, while the R226 was intended for 36ft-long bodywork with up to 52 seats. The new Fords retained 12-volt

Left **An early Bedford VAM in the fleet of York Pullman. It has a Plaxton Panorama II body, which was plainer in appearance than the companion Panorama I and featured top-sliding windows as standard. It also had different side mouldings, although in reality there were few hard and fast rules about such things with some operators combining features from both Panorama models. It carries Vam badging, fitted to the rear of the flashing trafficator.** *Martin Llewellyn*

electrics. The main differences between the R226 and the Thames 36 were the more powerful engine, a bigger clutch, a single-speed rear axle (with two-speed axle as an option), a heavier duty front axle, and the adoption of power steering as standard (it had previously been optional).

In 1965 a new R226 with Duple Mariner body (as the Marauder had by then become, albeit without any noticeable design changes), cost £5,805 or with Plaxton Panorama body £5,920. The chassis was priced at £1,765. For comparison a PSU3/3 Leopard chassis left little change from £2,900, while a Reliance 590 cost £2,975, so there were considerable savings to be had in buying a Ford. The new models from Bedford and Ford arrived at a time when the speed limit for coaches was being further relaxed, from the 40mph set in 1961, to a more realistic 50mph from August 1966.

It wasn't just the motorway network which opened new links in the 1960s. Four major estu-

arial crossings opened around the middle of the decade. In Scotland new road bridges across the Forth and the Tay made possible faster links between Edinburgh and Aberdeen. The opening of the Severn Bridge saw quicker services from South Wales to Bristol and ultimately to London. And the tunnel under the River Thames at Dartford saw the creation of a new coaching pool, Dartford Tunnel Coachways, which involved three BET companies – East Kent, Maidstone & District and Southdown – along with Tilling subsidiary Eastern National. They ran a network of summer services from Clacton and Great Yarmouth to destinations in Kent, and from Essex to resorts on the south coast.

Plaxton's range was facelifted in 1964, in readiness for the 1965 season, with styling work being done by Ogle Design. The most distinctive model in the new line-up was known as the Panorama I, although it was in fact the fourth major incarnation of the Panorama body. This featured a ribbed stainless steel moulding which

ran below the windscreen and extended the length of the first bay on each side of the body where a thin moulding strip continued up to the roof to meet the scoop for the forced-air ventilation system. There were new side mouldings and a much improved grille too, creating a stylish and restrained coach which made most of the competition look just a bit fussy. Side mouldings at skirt level allowed that area to be painted in a contrasting colour, although some bodies retained the style of side moulding used on the previous generation of Panoramas.

This was retained on the Panorama II, which was a cleaner, no-frills design – and just that bit less striking. It was marginally cheaper – about 5 per cent less than the Panorama I – and was sometimes badged as the Vam when fitted to Bedford chassis (and, erroneously, on occasion when fitted to Fords too). Both body styles were offered across the available range of chassis – Bedford VAM and VAL, Ford R192 and R226, Leyland Leopard and AEC Reliance. The

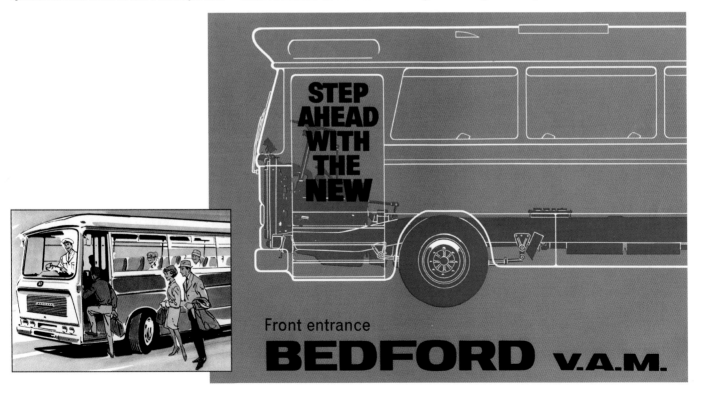

STEP AHEAD WITH THE NEW

Front entrance **BEDFORD** V.A.M.

Left **Two of Plaxton's new bodies at the 1964 Commerial Motor Show, showing the Ogle style adopted for 1965. Nearest the camera is a Bedford SB with Embassy IV body – compare the side mouldings with those on Barrie's Panorama-bodied Thames illustrated below. Next to it is a Leopard with Panorama I body, and alongside that, the rear of a Panorama II showing clearly the use of the same glass for front and rear windows.** *Plaxton*

Left below **Ogle's styling for the Panorama I was more radically different from the models which had gone before than was the Panorama II. The Panorama I was the more expensive model, with a distinctive waist-level polished moulding at the front and with forced-air ventilation as standard. Ribble took 32 Panorama Is in 1966 – 22 on PSU3 Leopards and 10 on Bedford VAM5s. The Leopards included eight for the Standerwick fleet. The Bedfords were sold in 1969 while the Ribble Leopards ran until 1976-77 before being transferred to other NBC fleets for further service.** *Martin Llewellyn*

Below **A 1965 Thames 570E operated by Barrie's of Balloch shows how the Panorama treatment was applied to bodies on front-engined chassis. This is a Panorama rather than an Embassy IV – the latter had opening side windows and different body mouldings, as shown on the artist's impression at the bottom of the page. The new body continued throughout the 1960s with little change on Bedford SB chassis, but its availability on the Thames was brief because Ford axed the 570E when it launched the R-series at the end of 1965.** *Harry Hay*

Panorama Type Body

Bedford VAS was only offered with a Panorama II body, but a new Embassy IV body was made available on the Bedford SB and, briefly, on the Thames 570E, with bigger windows and a similar grille to that used on the rest of the range. The Embassy IV had top-sliding windows; add fixed windows and polished mouldings which echoed the Panorama I styling theme and the new body became simply the Panorama on the SB and the 570E. The only major carry-over from the Embassy III to the Embassy IV/Panorama was the front windscreen.

Duple made some minor changes to its popular Bella range of bodies for 1965, applying the simplified N-type mouldings to the entire range. This was the year in which Duple delivered its 25,000th body – a Bella Vega on a Bedford SB for George Ewer.

European influences

One familiar name disappeared from coach manufacture in 1966 – Harrington. Thomas Harrington of Hove had been building bodies since 1897. Perhaps its most famous coach designs were those incorporating the so-called dorsal fin in the late 1940s and early 1950s. This distinctive vertical fin at the rear of the roof was used as an air extractor.

Harrington was owned by the Rootes group – makers of Hillman, Humber, Sunbeam and Singer cars, and of Commer commercials – and it was in need of investment which Rootes could ill afford. The move by operators to 36ft-long coaches had put severe pressure on the company's facilities, making it difficult to increase output.

When production ceased, the company was building three models, the classic Cavalier and Grenadier on AEC Reliance and Leyland Leopard chassis, and the square-rigged Legionnaire on 36ft-long Fords and Bedfords. The metal-framed Legionnaire lacked the confident touch of the previous generation of Harrington designs and from some angles looked a bit like Duple's Commander.

Harrington had also announced bodywork for the Bedford VAM which, had it appeared, would have been a shortened – 32ft 4in – Legionnaire. One unusual Legionnaire-style body deserves a mention. Guy had quietly disappeared from the British coach market at the end of the 1950s, but one solitary Victory chassis – an export model – was bodied by Harrington in 1965 and delivered to Hereford-based Penn Overland Tours. Penn operated trans-continental tours to India, and the Victory was air-conditioned.

The company's output had been in the order of 180 coaches a year and it had a steady following among the BET group. BET buyers of Harrington bodies in the early 1960s included local operator Southdown which bought 62 Cavaliers, East Yorkshire, Hebble, North Western, Maidstone & District, Northern General, Ribble (another big user, with 57 delivered in 1961/63), South Wales Transport, Trent, Western Welsh and Yorkshire Woollen. Other well-known buyers included Black & White, the George Ewer group, Silver Star, Timpson, Valliant Direct and Yelloway. The last Harrington body was a Grenadier for Greenslades' Tours of

Exeter, an 80-vehicle coach-operating subsidiary of BET.

Duple continued refining the range which it had introduced in 1962. There had been minor changes in 1965, while for 1966 new grilles and body side mouldings were introduced and the range rationalised following the introduction of the Bedford VAM and Ford R192 in place of the SB5 and Thames Trader. The range now comprised five models which retained the reverse rake pillar towards the rear (this was to be its last season), and two which did not. Those with the reverse rake pillar were the Vega Major on the Bedford VAL, the Mariner on the Ford R226, the outwardly similar Empress and Bella Venture on the Ford R192 and Bedford VAM respectively, and the diminutive Bella Vista on the Bedford VAS. The Empress and Bella Venture were new for 1966 and lasted just one season.

The two bodies which had vertical pillars for their full length – and bigger side windows too – were the Commander, on AEC Reliance, Leyland Leopard and Daimler Roadliner, and the new Viscount on Bedford VAM and Ford R192. Both

Left **The styling of Harrington's Legionnaire was softened slightly from 1964 with the adoption of curved cove panels in place of the original angular style illustrated on the Barton VAL on page 60. In its new guise it was known as the Legionnaire II and was rather more attractive, looking not unlike Duple bodies of later in the decade. A Thames 36, owned by Lewis Cronshaw but in Aer Lingus colours, waits at London's Heathrow Airport.** *Harry Hay*

Right top **Harrington offered two bodies on 36ft-long underfloor-engined chassis, the Cavalier and the Grenadier. Valliant of Ealing bought this Cavalier which had a Grenadier-style front. It was one of three on AEC Reliance 590 chassis.** *Maurice Bateman*

Right **Greenslades of Exeter was a tour operator and part of the BET group. It ran a fleet of 80 coaches. To allow operation over the narrow roads on Dartmoor some of these were built to a width of 7ft 6in long after 8ft or even 8ft 2½in had become the norm. Deliveries in 1964 included Harrington-bodied Reliances built to the narrow width. This Cavalier incorporates a Grenadier-style lower front panel – there were few firm rules in coachbuilding in the 1960s.** *Maurice Bateman*

Viscount

Above **The Vega Major body for the Bedford VAL was updated in line with the rest of the Duple range, as was the Mariner, visible in the background of this shot of two coaches owned by Campings of Brighton. The body on the Ford R226 is higher built and also incorporates glazed cove panels, an option on most Duple bodies in the early part of the 1960s.** *Stewart J Brown*

Left **The Viscount was built at Blackpool in 1966-67 for the Bedford VAM and Ford R192, competing for orders with the Hendon-built Bella Venture and Empress in 1966, and with the new Viceroy in 1967.**

Left above **Duple updated its range for 1966 with new grilles and side trim. Whether or not the changes were an improvement is open to debate. For the new Bedford VAM Duple extended its Bella range with the Bella Venture. This retained the reverse rake pillar towards the rear, but incorporated the new grille style. As with the Bella Vega/Trooper models, a distinction was made between identical bodies mounted on Bedford and Ford chassis, with the R192's body being called the Empress. Both the Empress and the Bella Venture were only offered for the 1966 coaching season. This is a VAM14 in the South Midland fleet.** *Iain MacGregor*

Left below **An AEC Reliance with the revised Commander body is seen in Dewsbury operating for Hebble. It is a short – nominally 32ft – model. Note that unlike the bodies on lightweight chassis illustrated above, the Commander has vertical pillars for its full length.** *Iain MacGregor*

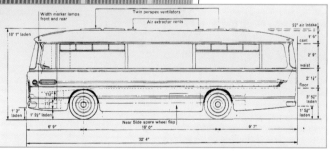

Duple Viscount
45 passenger front entrance on Ford R192 chassis
32ft 4in x 8ft 2½ x 10ft 1in laden

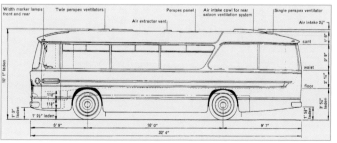

Duple Empress
45 passenger front entrance on Ford R192 chassis
32ft 4in x 8ft 2½ x 10ft 1in laden

Below **Scottish Omnibuses obtained permission to operate this left-hand drive Magirus-Deutz on its Edinburgh to London service in 1966. The 10m-long 41-seater had a rear-mounted engine and underfloor locker space. It is seen in Edinburgh prior to entering service. It didn't win Magirus-Deutz any orders.** *B J Keddie*

Bottom **After being exhibited at the 1966 Commercial Motor Show the Mercedes-Benz O.302 went on a demonstration tour. Scottish Omnibuses operated it between Edinburgh and London in the spring of 1967. The integral 43-seater is seen in Edinburgh. Note that the first three bays are of a different length from those at the rear.** *Travel Press*

the Commander and the Viscount were built at Blackpool in the former Burlingham works and made more use of steel in their framing than did the Hendon-built Bella family of bodies. The Commander had fixed windows and forced-air ventilation; on all of the other bodies top-sliding vents were fitted to the side windows. All full-size bodies now used the same windscreens, with the option of single or two-piece screens across the range. The Viscount name had previously been used by Willowbrook.

The first modern European-built coach to run in service in Britain did so in May 1966. This was a left-hand-drive Magirus-Deutz 150 L10, which operated under special dispensation from the traffic commissioners on the Edinburgh to London service of Scottish Omnibuses, complete with Edinburgh registration GFS948D. The 10m two-door 38-seater had a rear-mounted air-cooled 150bhp 9.5-litre Deutz V6 engine driving through an eight-speed manual gearbox. A report in *The Scottish Omnibus*, the staff magazine of the Scottish Bus Group, found one piece of equipment worth commenting on: "The speedometer/milometer is hinged, and underneath there is fitted a circular disc, upon which the length of each journey and duration of driving is marked. This method is virtually foolproof, and would seem to be a vast improvement on present checks on hours worked etc." The word tachograph was not yet in common currency.

The German-built Magirus-Deutz was operated alongside the latest generation of SBG London service coaches – Bristol RELH6Gs. These had been introduced to both the Scottish Omnibuses and Western SMT fleets in 1966 to replace the original 36ft-long Reliances and Leopards which were being downgraded to less arduous work. Like their predecessors they had Alexander Y-type bodies, but the REs had 150bhp Gardner 6HLX engines, giving a bit more power for the 400-mile run. The Y-type body had a restyled front panel, to provide a better flow of air to the RE's front-mounted radiator. A total of 65 of these coaches entered SBG service. The majority had 38 reclining seats and a toilet, but 12 were luxurious 40-seaters (at a time when 49 was the norm) for the two- and three-day tourist services which Scottish Omnibuses – now trading as Eastern Scottish – ran between Edinburgh and London.

At the 1966 Commercial Motor Show

Mercedes-Benz was back again. It showed an O.302, which entered demonstration service in 1967 with the apt registration OLH302E. The O.302 embodied a number of stereotypical Germanic qualities, being well-built but perhaps a bit austere. At £10,500 it was also expensive – you could buy a perfectly nice Plaxton-bodied Leyland Leopard for less than £8,000.

The O.302, introduced in Germany at the start of 1965, was an integral – something of a novelty to British eyes although common practice in Europe – and it had a rear-mounted 175bhp OM327 7.98-litre engine. Air-suspension was another interesting feature, and something else about which British operators still remained to be convinced, along with rear engines and integral construction. Had it been price competitive with home-built products the O.302 would have struggled to find a market. With a price premium of some 20 per cent it just didn't stand a chance.

The demonstrator did the rounds, visiting Tilling and BET operators, and running on the two-day Edinburgh to London service of Scottish Omnibuses, but secured no sales. It was bought by Whiteford's of Lanark who rather optimistically set up a sales company to act as sole Scottish agents for Mercedes coaches. Another O.302 appeared at the 1968 show, now priced at just under £10,000, but it fared no better. It was sold to Seamarks of Luton (already running rear-engined Panther coaches) and was modified by raising the gangway by five inches to eliminate the deep well, and by fitting Plaxton seats in place of the original Mercedes recliners, which increased capacity from 43 to 47 passengers. Seamarks ordered a second O.302, which was exhibited at the 1970 Earls Court show.

Another European manufacturer, Van Hool, took a full-page advert in *Commercial Motor's* 1966 Show issue which posed the question: "Who is Van Hool?" The advert illustrated two interesting vehicles, which had been supplied earlier in the year to Smiths of Wigan. These were based on left-hand-drive Leyland Olympic underframes, salvaged from a boatload of Olympic buses bound for Cuba which had sunk in the River Thames in 1964. With the running units reconditioned, the underframes were fitted with 44-seat coach bodies by Van

COMMERCIAL MOTOR September 23 1966

33

who is Van Hool?

A brand ? Yes, the brand "with the long H" that is to be seen on most Touring Coaches or buses, on any road, in almost any country.
A plant ? Of course ! A really modern plant of more than 5 acres. An average of 5 vehicles (buses, coaches, commercial vehicles) are produced daily. Which means 1 vehicle every 100 minutes !
A specialist ? Obviously, Van Hool is an unmatched specialist in the building of super-Touring Coaches specially conceived and designed to fulfill the particular requirements of tourists from overseas.
A "top seller" ? True ! Van Hool Touring Coaches are by far the "top sellers" since 5 years, in Belgium. And since 3 years in the whole Benelux. Besides, Van Hool exports to a great number of countries.
Something special ? Wait until you've seen our new models. They make the most modern fleet look outmoded. They bring you new pride... and new profits, too ! 75 % of all British tourists on the continent are transported (and delighted !) in Van Hool Touring Coaches ! Why not send in the coupon below ? You'll find out everything about Van Hool Vehicles.

Please fill in and forward to VAN HOOL & SONS, sprl Koningshooikt, Belgium

VAN HOOL & SONS sprl
Coach builders, Koningshooikt, BELGIUM

Please send me detailed documentation on your Touring Coaches.
NAME :
ADDRESS :
CITY :
COUNTRY :

Hool who were based in Belgium. They retained left-hand-drive, which meant that the passenger entrance had to be in mid-wheelbase. They were used mainly on continental tours. They were the first modern coaches in Britain to have imported bodies – a fact whose significance went totally unnoticed at the time.

Smiths of Wigan was becoming one of the big names in coaching in the north-west of England. In 1964 Smiths (and the associated Websters business) had been bought by Blundell of Southport. The Blundell group fleet then stood at 55 coaches and grew further in the following year with the acquisition of Hargreaves of Bolton. In 1968 it would add two associated Manchester businesses to its portfolio – Stanley Spencer and Happiway Tours – and by the start of the 1970s the group would be running almost 150 coaches.

Bottom **Both BEA and BOAC started running double-deckers to Heathrow in the 1960s. While BEA opted for bus-like Routemasters – under the influence of LT which was running them on BEA's behalf – BOAC ran its own fleet and was under no such constraints. Instead it chose Leyland Atlanteans with stylish 54-seat Metro-Cammell bodies. A fleet of 15 entered service in 1966. They ran until the late 1970s.** *Stewart J Brown*

AEC upgraded its Reliance range in 1966, phasing out the Reliance 470 in favour of the Reliance 505, and the 590 in favour of the 691. The 146bhp 8.2-litre AH505 engine was offered in chassis for 30ft and 36ft bodywork and with a choice of five- or six-speed synchromesh gearboxes, or the four-speed Monocontrol semi-automatic. The 11.3-litre AH691 offered no real increase in power, with quoted output up from 153 to 154bhp. From 1967 a five-speed Monocontrol gearbox was available as an option.

While the Ford R226 offered more power than the Thames 36, 128bhp was not particularly generous for a 36ft coach. A London operator, Whitefriars Coaches, addressed this problem in 1966 by having an R226 modified to accept a 166bhp 7.7-litre Cummins V8 engine and an Allison automatic gearbox. A Klam retarder was fitted – an idea ahead of its time – and the coach was intended for continental touring. This powerful Ford had a Plaxton Panorama I body.

The compact V-engine fitted below the floor level – unlike the Ford in-line six which protruded well above the floor, compromising the entrance layout. On a road test in *Bus & Coach* magazine it produced a record 0-30mph time of 14 seconds (an R192 with Ford's Turbo 360

engine took 19 seconds) and its open road fuel consumption was an impressive 15.25mpg (the R192 returned 16.1). It was also one of the fastest coaches tested by *Bus & Coach*, reaching 72mph, a figure equalled only by another Cummins-powered coach – the bigger-engined Daimler Roadliner.

Continental coach tours grew in popularity in the 1960s, with operators such as Excelsior of Bournemouth, Global Tours of London, LeRoy Tours of Tunbridge Wells and Southdown all buying coaches for use on tours to Europe. LeRoy set up a maintenance facility at Innsbruck, while Excelsior had its own depot in Ostend.

London's Victoria Coach Station was used primarily by Tilling and BET operators, but in 1967 Grey-Green, Suttons of Clacton and Eastern National pooled their resources on the London to Clacton operation, marketing the new joint services under the Essex Coast Express title. Grey-Green thus became the first independent to run regular services from Victoria. Co-operation between East Anglian operators was strengthened in 1968 when the East Anglian Express Services pool was formed to bring together and market the operations of

Eastern Counties, Eastern National and Grey-Green between London and Ipswich, Felixstowe and Great Yarmouth.

The growth in air travel in the 1960s saw a corresponding growth in demand for airport links, and nowhere was this more visible than at London's busy Heathrow Airport. British European Airways had been serving the airport with one-and-a-half-deck AEC Regal IVs, running from a terminal in west London at Gloucester Road. From the end of 1966 these were replaced by 65 forward-entrance Routemaster coaches which, like those operated on Green Line services, were really upgraded buses. To overcome the potential problem of carrying passengers' luggage, they towed trailers. Power was supplied by 175bhp AEC AV690 engines, making them Britain's most powerful double-deckers.

At the same time the British Overseas Airways Corporation, whose London terminal was just opposite Victoria Coach Station in Buckingham Palace Road, bought 15 Atlanteans with Metro-Cammell bodies. These had genuine coach seats for 54 passengers and had luggage accommodation at the rear of the lower saloon. One was exhibited at the 1966 Commercial Motor Show. BOAC also provided a coach link in Scotland, between its Glasgow terminal in St Enoch's Square and Prestwick Airport. Two 36ft Harrington-bodied Reliances operated this service from 1964, replacing earlier Harrington Contender integrals.

A number of coach operators, particularly in London and the south-east, had strong links with airlines and provided coaches to handle the growing numbers of holidaymakers heading abroad. Samuelson ran to Gatwick Airport, with coaches in the silver, blue and white colours of British United Airways which, from the early 1960s, replaced cream and green as Samuelson's fleet livery. Seamarks was the best-known of a number of operators serving Luton Airport.

MCW's dogged determination to sell coaches in the 1960s has to be admired. For Bedford's VAM and Ford's R-series chassis it produced the Athena, launched in 1966 and displayed in the demonstration park at that year's Commercial Motor Show. Like all MCW products, it had a steel frame and the company made great play of its low weight. In its 1966 Show issue *Commercial Motor* reported: "The Athena

MCW ATHENA
LUXURY WITH ECONOMY THROUGH GOOD DESIGN

Below **Arguably MCW's least successful 1960s coach – indeed possibly Britain's least successful 1960s coach – was the Athena. Built on a Bedford VAM5 chassis, it was an exhibit in the demonstration park at the 1966 Commercial Motor Show at Earls Court. That was as far as it got. MCW reworked it and it became the prototype for the Metropolitan, which was launched in 1967.**
Iain MacGregor

attention has been paid to complete design integration with respect to the visual balance of the coach, the new purposeful appearance of the front and rear end, and the overall paint proportions." Of the interior he said: "A new simplicity has been achieved by means of removing all unnecessary visual distractions and irregularity of form. This approach is in keeping with the best current thinking in jet aircraft travel; it is designed to leave the coach user free to appreciate the ride, comfort and journey, and at the same time induce a sense of well being." The interior styling was by David Bache, who had done design work for Rover cars. Between 1967 and 1969 MCW built 33 Metropolitan coaches, all on Bedford VAM chassis.

Among the few Metropolitan users were Smiths of Wigan with two on Leyland-engined VAM14s. Other buyers included Knightswood Coaches of Watford and Cook of Dunstable, both of whom took theirs to the 1967 British Coach Rally. Blue Saloon of Guildford bought one in 1968. The model was officially launched as the Metropolitan 32/41 – indicating nominal length and seating capacity – but the numbers were soon abandoned. The original intention had been to build the

coach body marks the return of MCW to the luxury coachbuilding field. Unfortunately not ready in time to appear inside Earls Court, this 41/45-seat coach on Bedford VAM chassis should be seen as the company is determined to enter this field of coachbuilding in a big way." It was the company's best effort yet, but once again made no impact on the market which was increasingly dominated by Duple and Plaxton. The Athena was also offered on the Bedford VAL, in place of the Topaz II, but no long Athenas were built.

Indeed even the standard Athena never actually entered service. Instead it was restyled and relaunched for 1967 as the Metropolitan on the VAM, but buyers were still few and far between. This despite the glowing description of MCW's chief engineer, T McConnell, who said: "Careful

Metropolitan at Weymann's Addlestone plant, but the closure of Addlestone saw the bulk of production being carried out at the Metro-Cammell factory at Elmdon.

In 1969 production of the Metropolitan was sub-contracted to Strachan, and at one stage there were plans for Strachan to build 85 Metropolitan bodies on Ford and Bedford chassis. In the end Strachan built only ten, all on Ford R192 chassis.

The MCW Topaz II did appear on one other 36ft chassis – the Leyland Panther. Two were bought by BET subsidiary East Yorkshire in 1967. It was hardly a winning combination – MCW's coach body and Leyland's rear-engined Panther chassis – and both were relatively short-lived, being scrapped after nine years at a time when East Yorkshire's vehicles generally had a 13-year life. They were the last MCW coach bodies for a BET group company. East Yorkshire, incidentally, was the biggest user of the Panther coach chassis, taking 24 in all – the two Topaz IIs in 1967, three Plaxtons and four with Marshall dual-purpose bodies in 1968, plus 15 which had Marshall bus bodies..

Bristol had made no real impression on independent fleets, even though its RE had been available to them since a share exchange with Leyland in 1965 allowed Bristol products to be sold on the open market. Two with Leyland engines – a new option – and Plaxton bodies

were sold to independents in 1967, Flight of Birmingham and Byng of Portsmouth. And that was it as far as the RE was concerned in the private sector. These were, incidentally, the first Bristols to be sold to an independent operator for almost 20 years.

It was in 1967 that Bristol launched a new light mid-engined chassis, the LH, and with this it began to notch up a few sales to coach operators. There were three LH models – the short LHS, the standard LH, and the 11m LHL. A choice of Perkins H6.354 or Leyland O.401 engines was offered, driving through a Turner five-speed gearbox. The Perkins was rated at 101bhp and was offered only in the LHS and LH variants. The 125bhp Leyland unit was available on all three models, and was the only engine offered in the LHL. Most small operators favoured the Leyland option. All coach LHs were bodied by Duple and Plaxton. Four operators – including Byng again – bought a total of seven LH coaches in 1968. Sales to independents of the 10m LH rose to a peak of 12 in 1969, before falling back to eight in 1970.

The long-wheelbase LHL, the rarest model in the LH range, initially did fairly well with small operators with 65 in operation by the end of 1970. But here, too, sales tailed off and only nine entered service in 1971, followed by 15 in 1972 and ten in 1973. Most LHLs had Plaxton bodies, with just four being bodied by Duple.

The LHS, destined to be the longest-lived of the new light Bristols, did not figure in the private sector coach market until 1974.

The LH range did not do very well as a public sector coach either. Thames Valley took eight with Duple bodies in 1968-69. The only other NBC subsidiaries to run LH coaches were Western National (also Duple-bodied) and, with Plaxton bodies, United Auto and Cumberland. All except a solitary LH6P for Cumberland had Leyland engines. North of the border it was tried by two SBG companies – Eastern Scottish and Alexander (Midland). The SBG LH coaches had Perkins engines and Alexander Y-type bodies, incorporating the rather severe frontal style first seen on the Group's 1966 Bristol REs. There were 38 for Alexander (Midland), delivered between 1970 and 1972, and 34 for Eastern Scottish, all new in 1970 with 38-seat bodies. After the LH Alexander (Midland) turned to Fords, while Eastern Scottish switched to Bedfords.

Bedford stopped fitting Leyland engines in 1967, with the introduction of its new 70-series 466cu in (7.6-litre) engine, originally seen in 1966 in the KM 16-ton truck range. This appeared in the VAM70 and the VAL70, replacing not only Leyland engines, but also the Bedford 330cu in unit used in the VAM5. At the same time the VAS was given the 330 engine in place of the 300cu in, changing from being the

Left **The MCW Metropolitan was a marked improvement on the Athena. The basic structure was the same but with much simpler side mouldings and a new front end, the ugly duckling Athena was transformed into something approaching a swan. The use of rectangular headlights was innovative. Elm Park Coaches of Romford was an early customer for the Metropolitan, taking this one in the spring of 1967 on a Leyland-engined VAM14.** *Trevor Brookes*

This Bristol LH lightweight chassis has a bus on its back all day long

Over 400 L.H. lightweights have been bought for use as bus chassis. That's the measure of operators' confidence in the L.H.'s ability to withstand wear and tear.
It follows that as a coach chassis the L.H. must be very reliable (the experience of over 30 operators bears this out).
The L.H. lightweight offers you underfloor engine mounting which drastically reduces interior noise and simple chassis design that keeps maintenance simple.

By contrast, carrying a coach is a holiday

Also, you'll have full air brakes and a spring actuated parking brake controlled by a small lever in the driver's cab.
These features may not be suprising in themselves but you *will* be surprised when you discover the low price you're asked to pay for the L.H. Independent road test figures and report will be supplied on request.
For all the details, contact Bristol Commercial Vehicles Ltd., Bath Road, Bristol BS4 3LD
Telephone : 77613

BRISTOL

Bottom **Duple modified the Commander body to fit the Bristol LH chassis for a batch of 12 coaches delivered to Western National in 1970 for the Royal Blue fleet. These were 41-seaters on Leyland-engined LH6L chassis. The only other operator of Duple-bodied LHs at this period was Thames Valley.** *Stewart J Brown*

VAS1 to the VAS5. Although lightweight coaches had got bigger and heavier, they were still surprisingly light – a VAM70 with Plaxton Panorama body, for example, weighed just over 6 tons – 6 tons 0 cwt 2 qrs was a typical legal weight – which was not at all bad for a 45-seater.

The VAM70 became Bedford's standard 10m coach – but one operator was still buying a rare beast indeed, the petrol-engined VAM3. Salopia Saloon Coaches was sticking to its belief that petrol engines were far superior to diesels for touring coaches, something which few would argue with but which no other operator would countenance because of the high running costs. In 1968 it tried diesel power, taking three diesel-engined VAMs alongside its seven new VAM3s. In 1969 all 12 new VAMs were petrol-engined, and 1970's new coach intake comprised seven petrol-engined SB3s and two diesel-engined VAM70s. It was a remarkable example of an operator sticking to its principles. The sight of a G-registered Duple Viceroy purring into a coach park must really have turned other drivers' heads – if they heard it coming.

In 1971 all changed and Salopia was taken over by Bee-Line of West Hartlepool. And that was the end of petrol-engined coaches.

Bigger coaches were in the news once again in 1967, with a further relaxation of the limits on maximum length – up from 11m to 12m – although it would be 1968 before any 12m coaches took to Britain's roads and the move by operators from 11m to 12m would be much more gradual than that from 30ft to 36ft earlier in the decade. Leyland responded to the revised legislation with a new PSU5 Leopard, and AEC with a longer Reliance.

For the 1967 season Duple was still tinkering with its coach range. The Commander and Viscount continued unchanged, but the remaining models were rationalised further and the distinctive reverse rake pillar which had been adopted in 1962 was finally abandoned on all models except the low-volume Bella Vega on the Bedford SB5 chassis. The Bella Vista was restyled to match the Commander and Viscount, and renamed the Vista 25 – its 24ft 9in overall length rounded up to the nearest foot.

A new Viceroy body was introduced at the 1966 Show for the VAM and R192, with the Viceroy 36 for the VAL and R226. This retained

Left top **Having facelifted its existing bodies for 1966, Duple unveiled the new Viceroy for 1967. This was all-new – apart from the grille – and was launched at the 1966 Commercial Motor Show. It replaced the Mariner, Vega Major, Empress and Bella Venture on Bedford and Ford chassis. A Ford R192 demonstrator illustrates Duple's new look. The deep side windows were a major step forward.** *Iain MacGregor*

Below **The Viceroy did not initially replace Duple's Commander. The Commander III adopted the Viceroy windscreen and had an attractive new grille which foreshadowed changes coming to the Viceroy range. A 1968 Maidstone & District Leopard awaits the return of its passengers on a damp summer day in Fort William.** *Iain MacGregor*

Bottom **Although body specifications were gradually becoming more standardised, there was still some flexibility. Hants & Dorset took three Commander III bodies in 1968 which had glazed cove panels and top-sliding windows. They were also unusual in being on Bristol RE chassis.** *Martin Llewellyn*

the radiator grille first used on the 1966 models, but everything else was new. The side windows were big and deep, with a separate top section where on previous generations of coaches there had been gently curved cove panels. This made the interior considerably brighter, without the cost of adding curved glass cove windows. The single-piece front windscreen was new, with more wrap-round, and there was a distinctive forward-sloping pillar above the rear of the front wheelarch. A peak above the windscreen housed the destination display. All this came at a cost, of course. The Vega Major body, for example, had carried a list price of £3,995 while the new Viceroy 36 on the Bedford VAL cost £4,280 – a seven per cent increase at a time of low inflation. Underneath the skin Duple retained composite construction.

One batch of Commanders was built which incorporated a Viceroy-like peaked front dome and separate flat-glass panels above the main body side windows. This was the Commander II and it was an unhappy amalgam of Duple designs. Just four were built, on Bristol RESH chassis for Hants & Dorset. For the 1968 season the Commander was given a facelift, with a neat new grille which was in fact a foretaste of even greater changes to come. In this short-lived guise it was called the Commander MkIII and was offered on a wider range of chassis – AEC Reliance, Leyland Leopard, Daimler Roadliner and two variants of Bristol's rear-engined coach, the 36ft RELH and the 32ft 7in RESH.

The RESH, incidentally, proved to be the least popular variant of the Bristol range and only 11 were built – the four Hants & Dorset coaches in 1967, followed by five Duple-bodied vehicles in 1968 for Eastern National and Southern Vectis. The other two were ECW-bodied dual-purpose vehicles for Midland General.

The vast majority of the popular RELH model were bodied by ECW for Tilling and NBC

Left **On the Bedford VAL the new Duple body was initially styled Viceroy 36. Most were supplied to independents, but a few were bought by Tilling companies and subsequently operated by NBC. A former Wilts & Dorset Viceroy 36, still in its original livery but with NBC-style Hants & Dorset fleet name, leaves Victoria Coach Station in the summer of 1973. The tartan seat covering was typical of the period.** *Stewart J Brown*

From Duple's 1970 brochure, a view of the
finishing shop at Hendon with a Commander on
the left and a Viceroy in the centre. Body
production at Hendon had ceased during 1969.

subsidiaries, but a few Tilling companies speci-
fied Duple bodies. In 1968 Hants & Dorset took
Duple bodies on five coaches while Thames
Valley took four. These were followed by two
more for Hants & Dorset in 1969 and a pair for
Eastern National in 1970. These numbers – 13
Duples over three years – have to be seen
against deliveries of over 200 ECW-bodied
RELH coaches to Tilling/NBC companies over
the same period.

The last examples of ECW's original style of
coach body for the RE were delivered in the
spring of 1970. The body was substantially
unchanged from that first seen in 1962, the
main change being a longer front overhang from
1968 on bodies built on Series II RE chassis on
which the front axle was set further back. There
were detail differences in destination displays to
suit individual operator's needs, and vehicles
which were considered to be primarily express
coaches had a two-piece door in place of the
single-piece door fitted to true coaches.

Improvements in bodies often brought
increased weight, and on mid-engined coaches
the load capacity of the front axle was at times a
problem. Duple's new Commander tipped the
balance (almost literally) on the short-wheel-
base AEC Reliance which required the fitment of
heavier duty springs to cope. Sometimes the
problem was identified only after the chassis
had been bodied, requiring remedial work
before the complete coach was delivered to its
end user.

Duple was still building coaches at two locations – the original factory in Hendon and the
former Burlingham works in Blackpool. As the
range was rationalised, so too were production
facilities, and in the summer of 1968 Duple
announced that it would be ceasing coach manufacture at Hendon. Property values were considerably higher in London than in Lancashire,
and so to were labour rates. During the ensuing
12 months all body building activities were
transferred to Blackpool.

Rationalisation among operators

The structure of the bus industry was changing. In 1968 the BET group sold its UK bus operations to the state-owned Transport Holding Company. The 1968 Transport Act set further change in motion. It created the National Bus Company in England and Wales, which was formed on 1st January 1969 and took over the operations of the THC and former BET fleets. It slowly welded the two disparate organisations together. The 1968 Act also created Passenger Transport Executives in the four major English conurbations – Tyneside, Merseyside, West Midlands and Greater Manchester. In the last-named the South East Lancashire North East Cheshire PTE took over the coach fleet of Manchester City Transport and, reforming it as SELNEC Travel, set about expanding its coach operations. In Scotland the Scottish Bus Group came under the control of a new Scottish Transport Group.

The 1968 Commercial Motor Show saw new bodies from Plaxton and another update from Duple. Plaxton broke new ground with its Panorama Elite range, which used curved glass side windows for the first time in a British coach. These extended up to the shallow roof and were mounted in rubber gaskets for ease of replacement. Inside, much more use was made of Formica trim, in place of the traditional cloth finish.

In the Plaxton way the Panorama Elite was evolutionary – the front grille was carried over from the previous range – but it was quite a remarkable step forward and it set the style for British coaches for the 1970s. The same basic body was now applied to all full-size chassis without distinction, and the Elite marked the continuation of Plaxton's ascendancy over arch-rivals Duple. The Panorama Elite replaced the Panorama I immediately, but the Panorama II

with its flat glass side windows continued until 1970 with the last being a batch of 30 on Leyland Leopard chassis for Midland Red. The Panorama body on the Bedford SB and VAS continued with little change.

Duple's two-year-old Viceroy was restyled by consultants Olsen Design to quite dramatic effect. The purposeful-looking Viceroy 37 – the longer of the two models had been stretched

The design which set the seal on Plaxton's success was the Panorama Elite, with its gently curved side windows. An early user was Cotter of Glasgow, with this 47-seat Leyland Leopard in the company's distinctive livery. The grille was a carry-over from the previous Plaxton range, but all else about the Panorama Elite was new. *Iain MacGregor*

Below Plaxton revised the side mouldings on bodies fitted to the Bedford SB and VAS. But sales of both these models had fallen sharply from the mid-1960s onwards, and the body which was sold alongside the new Elite in the early 1970s was essentially that introduced in 1965. Sales volumes didn't justify the development of a new body. This 1967 Bedford SB was operated by MacBrayne. *Harry Hay*

Right above The final Olsen-styled version of the Viceroy was a purposeful-looking coach with its crisp lines and clean-cut grille. An Alexander (Northern) Ford R1014 passes through Caernarfon in 1973. A front-engined coach would not be the quietest or most relaxing mode of transport for a holiday tour from Aberdeen to Wales – but Fords were the most luxurious touring coaches in the Alexander (Northern) fleet. *Iain MacGregor*

Right below Best & Sons of Ealing bought the only AEC Sabre to operate in Britain. It had an ECW body, which foreshadowed the style to be adopted for the Bristol RELH, but was noticeably taller. By the time it appeared at the 1972 Brighton coach rally it had acquired Leyland Sabre badges. The rearmost row of seats was set high above the engine. *Geoff Mills*

Sabre had coil spring suspension and a five-speed Monocontrol semi-automatic gearbox. The home market VP2R model had a 19ft or 20ft wheelbase for bodywork of, respectively, 11m or 12m nominal overall length. AEC's 1968 publicity brochure showed a dramatic shot of a Duple Commander body, but that was wishful thinking on AEC's part. All that existed at this stage was a left-hand-drive chassis, which was at the 1968 Commercial Motor Show. AEC's advertising made much of the Sabre's long-distance potential with the quaint heading "To Edinburgh or Istanbul AEC V8 Sabre coach offers you an exciting new potential" – which even by the standards of headline writers was barely English.

It carried a hefty – and unrealistic – price premium, with the chassis costing £5,400 at a time when a 12m Reliance 691 cost £3,500. At the 1970 Show there was a complete

from 36ft to just over 37ft – had a stylish new grille and a fluted stainless steel trim panel at wheelarch level which wrapped round the front of the coach to embrace the headlamps and a panel for the registration plate. The stainless steel theme was carried on in a ribbed moulding above the door which carried forward the line of the top window section. Rubber bumpers on the corners showed a touch of practicality. The interior was restyled too, with improved seats and new overhead luggage racks. Duple described the Viceroy as "the most exciting and advanced form of luxury travel in Europe", which might have been stretching a point – but it did look good, even if it was overshadowed by the new range from Plaxton.

The Viceroy was initially offered only on lightweight chassis – Bedford and Ford – while a similarly revamped Commander – now the Commander MkIV – was available not just on the AEC Reliance and Leyland Leopard, but also on the Bristol LH and RESH in lengths of around 32ft 8in, 36ft 3in and 39ft 4in – or 12m, the new legal maximum. The last-named could hold up to 57 seats. The Commander MkIV was also listed on the Daimler Roadliner, although

none were built. The Viceroy 37 was later offered on heavyweight chassis too, as an alternative to the low-volume Commander which was withdrawn from production in 1970. The short Viceroy was briefly called the Viceroy 32.

The new grille was adapted for the Vista 25 for the 1970 season, and at the same time the Bella Vega was replaced by the Vega 31, thus completing the updated Duple range. Before adopting Olsen Design's styling, other possibilities were considered, including an angular design with deep side windows surmounted by shallow top-sliders, in a body which had the air of the last of the pre-Elite range of Plaxton Panoramas.

Another 1968 launch was Britain's most powerful coach yet – the AEC Sabre. This featured a rear-mounted 12.1-litre AEC V8 800-series engine which produced an impressive 247bhp at a time when the Reliance was on offer with a maximum of just 154bhp. The

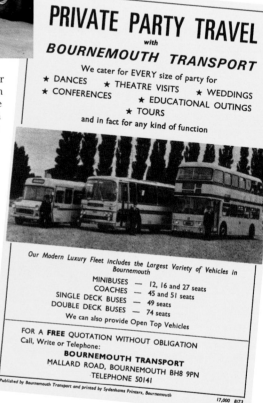

PRIVATE PARTY TRAVEL
with
BOURNEMOUTH TRANSPORT
We cater for EVERY size of party for
★ DANCES ★ THEATRE VISITS ★ WEDDINGS
★ CONFERENCES ★ EDUCATIONAL OUTINGS
★ TOURS
and in fact for any kind of function

Our Modern Luxury Fleet includes the Largest Variety of Vehicles in Bournemouth

MINIBUSES	— 12, 16 and 27 seats
COACHES	— 45 and 51 seats
SINGLE DECK BUSES	— 49 seats
DOUBLE DECK BUSES	— 74 seats

We can also provide Open Top Vehicles

FOR A **FREE** QUOTATION WITHOUT OBLIGATION
Call, Write or Telephone:
BOURNEMOUTH TRANSPORT
MALLARD ROAD, BOURNEMOUTH BH8 9PN
TELEPHONE 50141

Published by Bournemouth Transport and printed by Sydenhams Printers, Bournemouth

17,000 8/73

right-hand-drive Sabre, with a stylish 46-seat ECW body – ECW was by this time associated with AEC under the British Leyland umbrella. The ECW body on the Sabre was a precursor of a style to appear on the Bristol RE for NBC companies in the early 1970s. The launch Sabre was in fact the only UK Sabre. The "exciting new potential" never became reality. The Sabre's V8 800-series engine was offered in the Daimler Roadliner in 1969 (British Leyland had acquired Daimler in 1968) but was then abandoned by BL and the Sabre quietly disappeared. Before it did, there were plans to market it as the Leyland Sabre – but comments about deckchairs and the Titanic come to mind in relation to the activities of BL's marketing department. The ECW-bodied coach was bought by Best & Sons of Ealing. It entered service with an Oldham registration, reflecting the fact that its sale had been handled by Lancashire Motor Traders.

The new bodies from Plaxton and Duple overshadowed another new product – from Portugal. In 1967 Willment of Twickenham, a Ford dealer, imported two Caetano coach bodies, one on an R226 and the other a 25-seater on a modified D500 truck chassis. The R226 was sold to nearby Hounslow Coaches, while the D500 was bought by Hicks of Accrington. The idea had potential and in 1968 was taken up by a bigger coach dealer, Moseley, and marketed as the Moseley Continental.

93

Below **The first generation of Caetano bodies to be sold in the UK were square-cut and had highly-decorative grilles which for some observers invited comparison with juke boxes. All bodies were of generally similar appearance; this is an Estoril on a Bedford VAL running for Leamland of Horsted Keynes.** *Stewart J Brown*

From 1969 Wallace Arnold's coaches – except those based in Devon — carried a new Ogle-designed two-toned grey livery, which replaced the all-over cream in use since the start of the 1950s. A 1973 Leyland Leopard with Plaxton Panorama Elite body shows the new look. It carries the name of Gillards of Normanton, a small business acquired in 1968, and is seen on tour in Lochgilphead.

Harry Hay

The Portuguese styling was garish by British standards, and the interior trim unusual, with extensive use of plastics rather than moquette. An early example was fitted to a Leyland Leopard chassis and appeared in the demonstration park at the 1968 Commercial Motor Show in the livery of R&S Travel of London. The first generation of Caetano bodies was named after Portuguese places: Cascais, Estoril, Sintra and Lisboa, the country's capital. The Lisboa was for 36ft-long heavyweight chassis; the Estoril for the Bedford VAL and Ford R226; the Cascais for the VAM and R192; and the Sintra for the VAS5. At the 1969 British Coach Rally five Caetano-bodied coaches were entered – three Bedford VAMs, one VAL and a Leyland Leopard for Tatlock's, the well-known Lancashire operator – and by the time of the 1970 Commercial Motor Show Caetano had really come of age with coaches inside the Earls Court exhibition hall and not just in the demonstration park. In 1969 Moseley was quoting £7,556 for a Bedford VAL70/Estoril and £6,805 for a VAM70/Cascais.

Plaxton's new Panorama Elite was announced in time to be fitted to two batches of Daimler Roadliners for Black & White. Ten SRP8s, with 170bhp Perkins V8.510 engines in place of the troublesome Cummins units of earlier batches, entered Black & White service in 1969 followed by a further 10, also Perkins-powered, in 1970. These H-registered coaches were Britain's last Roadliners. A total of 54 Roadliners were bodied as coaches – 38 for Black & White, 15 for other operators, and a demonstrator. The other operators included three who had been Freeline users, Central of Walsall, Red House of Coventry and Blue Bus of Willington. In 1968 Daimler was quoting a Roadliner SRP8 chassis price of £3,468 with option prices which included:

air suspension	£220
power-assisted steering	£136
two-speed axle	£85
dual headlamps	£4 12s
engine revolution counter	£20
high water temperature warning device	£6 9s.

Winter Programme of
SIGHTSEEING TOURS
AND
COMPLETE TRAVEL SERVICES

OPERATED BY
EVAN EVANS TOURS
LIMITED
72/73 RUSSELL SQUARE, LONDON, W.C.1.   01-837 5544 or 0722

The basic list price was not that different from a Leyland Leopard with a semi-automatic gearbox.

Two Roadliners operated by Evan Evans

Tours of London were among early examples of what came to be known as executive coaches. Named Black Knight and Quicksilver, each had reclining seats – 27 in one, 30 in the other – tables and a bar. They had bodies by Plaxton and Duple respectively.

Evan Evans operated 38 coaches and was bought by Wallace Arnold in 1969, giving the expanding Leeds company its strongest-ever presence in the south. At that point Evan Evans had a further five Roadliners on order, which were promptly cancelled by the company's new owners. This happened as Wallace Arnold was adopting a new look with a two-tone grey livery and orange WA logo – all designed by Ogle – replacing the company's traditional cream. Much of Evan Evans business was built on transporting the growing numbers of tourists visiting London and arriving by air at Heathrow. This incoming tourist market provided new opportunities for a number of businesses such as Armchair Passenger Transport, Guards of London, R&S Travel, Charles Rickards Tours and World Wide Coaches.

While Bedfords and Fords were largely being bought by independents, a few did find their way into Tilling group coach fleets. Wilts & Dorset had bought five Bedford SB13s with Leyland engines and Duple bodies in 1965. These were followed by five VAM14s with Duple Viscount bodies in 1967, and then by 11 VAL70s, shared with the associated Hants & Dorset company, in 1968-69. These were used primarily on excursion work and on the movement of troops based on Salisbury Plain.

SBG companies also bought small numbers of Bedfords. Alexander (Midland) took 15 VAM5s in 1967 with Duple Viceroy bodies, adding a touch of luxury to the company's coach fleet in which Y-types had hitherto been the front-line vehicles. At the same time Central SMT took five similar vehicles for its small coach fleet, where they replaced 12-month-old Albion Vikings. Central had previously been buying Duple-bodied SB5s at the rate of five a year. Alexander (Northern) took a pair of Duple-bodied VAM70s in 1968, with more following in 1970. Highland Omnibuses opted for the unusual combination of Bedford VAM chassis and Alexander Y-type coach bodywork. Six were delivered in 1967 in Highland's blue and grey coach livery which had been inspired by the colours on a two-year-old Thames coach acquired from Happiways of Manchester in 1966.

One of the main attractions of 12m coaches was to provide increased carrying capacity on express services. Among the early users of the type was Premier Travel of Cambridge, with two Alexander Y-types on AEC Reliance chassis in May 1969. These had 53 seats instead of the 49 fitted to the company's existing 11m Y-types. More would follow. The 12m Y-type was an unusual coach – Premier Travel and Hebble were the only buyers.

For 12m operation Alexander was to produce something completely different – the M-type. This was developed specifically for use on SBG's motorway services from Glasgow and Edinburgh to London. The M-type was a high-floor body built on the Bristol REMH6G chassis. It had shallow double-glazed windows – a British first – to provide insulation on night services. The trapezoidal windows were sized and spaced to match the seat pitch. There were five main side windows and 10 rows of seats (plus two at the rear alongside the toilet, to make a total of 42). Other unusual fittings included an oil-fired Webasto heater, polished moulding strips on the body side, and roof-mounted marker lights front and rear. They had illuminated fleet name panels on the side (a feature carried over from the Y-type coaches used on Anglo-Scottish services) and were without a doubt the most distinctive coaches on regular service in Britain. Initial orders called for 24 – 16 for Western SMT and eight for Scottish Omnibuses. All entered service in 1969, further improving standards on the Scottish Bus Group's most prestigious routes. An interesting feature of the M-type was that it used the standard Y-type windscreen and rear windows, thus avoiding the cost of having expensive new screens made for what was a low-volume product. When M-type production ended in 1976 Alexander had built 98, including one rebody for Western SMT.

NBC, too, would try the 12m REMH6G, but with rather more conventional bodywork by Plaxton. They were bought by United Auto for

Above **The Alexander M-type was an impressive coach for its time. Built for operation on SBG services from Scotland to London, the M-type pioneered double-glazing in Britain and offered 42 passengers a high standard of comfort on the run to the capital. The initial vehicles were built on 12m-long Bristol REMH6G chassis for Western SMT and Eastern Scottish. The latter adopted a new pale yellow and black livery. Two M-types load in Edinburgh in August 1970.** *Iain MacGregor*

Right above **Plaxton won a number of orders to supply coach bodies on Bristol RE chassis to NBC subsidiaries. This is a 1971 RELH6L which had been ordered by Devon General, was delivered to Greenslades and is running on hire to Bristol Greyhound. The white livery with a broad coloured waistband was a short-lived identity adopted for coaches running to the West Country. The Bristol Greyhound version, using pink relief, can be seen on the ECW-bodied RE behind. The location is Victoria Coach Station in 1973; all would soon be replaced by National white.** *Stewart J Brown*

Right below **Many Tilling, and later NBC, companies took delivery of Bristol REs which had coach seats fitted in an ECW body using the basic bus shell. In 1972 Red & White received 13 RELH6Gs of this type. These were 47-seaters and one is seen leaving Cheltenham for Tenby when just a few months old. In some NBC fleets bodies of this style would receive all-over National white, although most companies opted to use the two-colour local coach livery for what were in essence dual-purpose vehicles.** *John Aldridge*

its London services with an initial tranche of 10 in 1971 being joined by a further 15 in 1973 and 10 Leyland-engined REMH6Ls in 1974. These were NBC's only REMHs and were being bought at a time when Plaxton's Elite body was winning a sizeable share of NBC's business on the more common 11m RELH chassis. In 1971-72 Plaxton supplied 68 bodies to a wide variety of NBC subsidiaries, following this up with 76 in 1973 and 45 in 1974. The last Plaxton-bodied REs were built in 1975; subsequent NBC coaches were Leopards. Ironically, the very last RELH chassis was bodied by Plaxton for an independent, Davies of Halewood. The only other REs for English independents had been a pair bodied by Plaxton back in 1967 when Bristols first became available on the open market.

The bodies which Plaxton and, to a lesser extent Duple, had supplied to Tilling/NBC on the RE were rather more stylish than ECW's body, which had been passably attractive at the start of the 1960s but was looking distinctly pedestrian by the end of the decade. In 1972 a new ECW coach body was unveiled, with deep flat-glass side windows and a deep curved windscreen similar to that used by Plaxton. It was a development of the body built on the AEC Sabre which had been shown at Earls Court in 1970.

In fact only 85 were built for NBC in two batches for delivery in 1972 and 1974. When deliveries started, the new coaches left ECW in individual company liveries, but this was the year when NBC's corporate identity was introduced and later vehicles were all over white with tiny company names over the front wheel-arches. The original design was 11m long, but to provide increased leg room some of the 1972 coaches plus all of those built in 1974 had the

rear overhang lengthened slightly. The extra length was incorporated in thicker rear corner pillars. The only buyer outside NBC for ECW's new coach body was the SELNEC PTE and its successor, the Greater Manchester PTE. SEL-NEC took 10 in 1973 and Greater Manchester placed a repeat order for 12 in 1975. These were built on mid-engined Leyland Leopard chassis and the rear sections of the body proved to be insufficiently strong and had to be rebuilt by the PTE. The body had, of course, been designed for a rear-engined chassis.

For real high capacity there was nothing to rival the double-decker and the first of a new generation of double-deck motorway coaches entered service with Standerwick in December 1968, running between Blackpool and London. This was a Bristol VRL, which had been one of the stars of the 1968 Commercial Motor Show.

The original fleet of Atlantean coaches had served the company well, but they were nearing the end of their front-line lives. Their replacements used the 36ft-long Bristol VRL/LH chassis, unusual in having the vertical Leyland O.680 engine mounted longitudinally behind the rear offside wheelarch. An attractive aluminium-framed body was built by Eastern Coach Works with 60 reclining seats – 42 upstairs and 18 down. This was 10 more seats than on the Atlanteans. The entrance was positioned just ahead of the rear wheels and the staircase was opposite it. This gave lower-deck passengers a better forward view than on the Atlanteans. There was a toilet at the rear of the lower saloon, and a large luggage locker.

Reliability, not a strong point on early Bristol VRT buses, was equally a problem on the VRL coaches and in-service breakdowns were not

uncommon. This could prove a headache for any companies called upon to provide a replacement vehicle. No other NBC company had 60-seat coaches, so if a fully-laden VRL broke down somewhere remote from its base the option was to provide either two coaches (which meant finding an extra driver) or a double-deck bus. By 1972 there were 30 VRLs in the Standerwick fleet but they were short-lived. Their handling at speeds in cross-winds was criticised, and one was involved in an accident in which it toppled over. All were withdrawn in 1974, some by then in National Travel corporate white. Indeed the last one to be delivered wore this livery from new.

Rather more mundane double-deck coaches of this period were being added to the fleets serving Heathrow Airport. Silverline of Hounslow took a trio of new Roe-bodied Atlantean coaches for operation on a Trans World Airlines contract in 1969, running between Heathrow and the TWA terminal in Kensington. These were long-wheelbase PDR2/1s with bodies featuring panoramic windows and based on a design being supplied to Leeds City Transport. Two years later BOAC added six Roe-bodied PDR2/1 coaches to its London fleet. These had a later style of Roe body, but still with distinctive panoramic windows. Both operators specified luggage storage space at the rear of the lower saloon. As Silverline's airport business expanded, it took another five Atlanteans in 1972, again Roe-bodied PDR2/1s. BOAC was also buying single-deck Leyland coaches, taking eight Plaxton-bodied Leopards in 1971, along with its six Atlanteans. These replaced six-year-old Duple-bodied Thames 36s.

Above left **In 1972 ECW built an attractive new coach body for the Bristol RE. This had deep flat-glass side windows, and an attractive Plaxton-style double-curvature windscreen set in a position which left space for a destination display above. Crosville received ten in the summer of 1972. These were delivered in the company's cream and black coach livery, but by the spring of 1973 work had already started on repainting them National white.** *Stewart J Brown*

Above **The only order to be placed for ECW coach bodies from outside NBC came from the SELNEC PTE and its successor, Greater Manchester. They took 22 on 11m Leyland Leopard chassis. They entered service in 1973 and 1975. A 1973 coach passes Ladybower.** *Martin Llewellyn*

Right **The 30 ECW-bodied Bristol VRLs operated by Standerwick were impressive coaches. They offered high carrying capacity – 60 people – and replaced the Gay Hostess Atlanteans on services from Lancashire to the south. One sets off from Blackpool's Coliseum coach station for Birmingham. National livery did not flatter the VRLs; they had looked altogether better in Standerwick cream and dark red.** *Malcolm King*

Below Silverline of Hounslow bought Atlantean coaches for airline contracts, specifying 33ft-long PDR2 chassis with Roe bodies of the style being built for Leeds City Transport. Five were delivered in 1972, but by 1973 this one was carrying the livery of Valliant, which had been taken over by Silverline. The Valliant Tavern name is appropriate for this private hire to the Derby, complete with wine glasses perched on the front upper-deck window sill. *Stewart J Brown*

Bottom For the Bedford YRQ, with its mid-mounted vertical engine, Duple had to raise the height of the Viceroy body as can be seen by comparing the location of the polished trim at wheelarch level with that on the Ford R1014 illustrated on page 92. The Tyneside PTE dabbled in coaching in 1971 and bought three Duple-bodied YRQs, one of which is seen in York. All three were sold at the end of 1972. This Viceroy has opening windows. *Chris Aston*

Right Mercedes-Benz made a number of

unsuccessful attempts to sell coaches in the UK in the 1960s and 1970s, trying with both complete integrals and with Plaxton-bodied O.302 underframes. The Plaxton body was lower-built than most Elites, and has a thicker pillar in mid-wheelbase. World Wide Coaches of London operated this one, which had been an exhibit at the 1969 Scottish Motor Show. It originally had the standard narrow Elite II polished side moulding but was later modified as seen here, with the wide Elite III moulding. *Stewart J Brown*

Silverline had become a major player in west London coaching, with a fleet of almost 100 vehicles. It had in 1970 taken over Valliant Cronshaw, which was the successor to Valliant Direct and Lewis Cronshaw, which had been combined in the ownership of Earls Court Holdings since 1966.

In 1969 Ford upgraded its increasingly popular R-series chassis, claiming 69 major improvements on the R192 and R226. The most significant change was the availability of a turbocharged version of the Ford 360 engine. This, the Turbo 360, offered 150bhp and was available in both chassis as an alternative to the 128bhp naturally-aspirated 360 unit. The 330 which had been standard on the R192 was dropped. The gross vehicle weights of both models were increased, allowing the fitment of bodies built to better (and consequently heavier) specifications. There were bigger brakes, improved suspension, new axles and the prices remained competitive. The R192 chassis cost £1,560, while the R226 was £1,850. Add the new Turbo 360 engine and these prices rose by £133.

The Turbo 360 was the first turbocharged engine to be offered as a production option on a British coach chassis available on the open market – the qualification is needed because Midland Red had of course pioneered the operation of coaches with turbocharged engines back in 1959.

Echoing the success of the company's Moscow run 10 years earlier, Ford sent an R226 on an even more ambitious trip in the autumn of 1968. A Turbo 360 model with Plaxton Panorama Elite body from the fleet of Excelsior Motorways of Bournemouth did a run from London to Bombay. In eight weeks it covered 14,000 miles at an average speed of 41.2mph and with an overall fuel consumption figure of 11.8mpg.

Bedford didn't take the challenge from Ford lying down. Its response to the improved R-series was to abandon the front-engined VAM70, replacing it with the underfloor-engined YRQ. This differed from other mid-engined chassis in that the engine was vertical, rather than horizontal. Engine and radiator were positioned behind the front axle. The use of a vertical truck engine kept costs down, but pushed the floor height up, as the top of the engine protruded above the chassis frame. The new layout was

made possible because of changes in the regulations relating to ground clearance and it gave Bedford the edge over Ford. The engine was the 150bhp 466cu in unit from the VAM70.

In tacit acknowledgement that front-engined coaches were noisy (and in a nice side-swipe at Ford), Bedford ran adverts under the headline: "The new mid-engine YRQ wins the noise battle foot down". The copy noted that the new engine position "keeps the noise element in its place – out of the saloon and completely below floor level".

For the YRQ Duple provided what it called the Viceroy Y-type – the Y-type appellation didn't catch on, which is perhaps not surprising since it had been associated with Alexander for the best part of 10 years. Before adapting the Viceroy to fit the new Bedford, Duple considered other alternative body styles, one of which had two banks of triple headlights. It used the fluted steel side trim of the Olsen-styled Viceroy, but located on the waist line, immediately below the windows, rather than at wheelarch level.

Mercedes-Benz was still interested in the British market and at the 1969 Scottish Motor Show tried a new tactic, showing an O.302 with Plaxton Panorama Elite body. This had a 185bhp 8.72-litre OM360 engine, five-speed synchromesh gearbox, air suspension and a Webasto auxiliary heater. It was exhibited in the livery of Whiteford's of Lanark (the aspiring

D—U—P—L—E

PROPOSED LUXURY COACH FOR 1970/71.
45 SEATER ON BEDFORD V.A.M. CHASSIS.
(UNDERFLOOR ENGINE)

Left top **The Mercedes integral was expensive, and whatever the value attached to the three-pointed star on the front, the body styling was unusual to British eyes, with relatively shallow high-set side windows. Operating as a courtesy coach at Heathrow Airport seems a menial task for a two-year-old high-priced continental coach. It was owned by World Wide Coaches.** *Stewart J Brown*

Left middle **With the owner at the wheel, the first Setra for a British operator pauses an Brighton's Madeira Drive during the 1972 British Coach Rally. It was new in August 1971 – and was still in service with Kirby's 27 years later.** *Geoff Mills*

Left bottom **Plaxton's Panorama Elite was fitted to all types of chassis and in the absence of badging there was often no clue as to what lay beneath. This 1971 coach is built on a Seddon Pennine IV chassis and was operated by Southern Coaches of Barrhead. The ventilation slots cut in the panel between the headlights were a feature of Elite bodies on Seddon and Bristol chassis. From 1971 the front grille was subtly modernised by aligning the top section with the main body side moulding; it had previously been a few inches higher. This was one of the distinguishing features of the Panorama Elite II.** *Iain MacGregor*

Scottish agents for Mercedes coaches), who already operated an O.302 integral, but was sold to World Wide Coaches of London. The Mercedes-Plaxton was priced at £11,750 – against £13,200 for a German-built integral O.302. The continuing rise in Mercedes prices was largely due to the strength of the German mark. A second Mercedes O.302/Plaxton was sold to Blueways of London in 1974.

Further attempts were made to promote the complete O.302 integral. Four were supplied to World Wide of London in 1971, while Grey-Green and Wallace Arnold each bought one. Seamarks of Luton ordered five, to join one bought new and an ex-demonstrator. By this time the price had shot back up, and was now in the region of £13,000.

A one-off import from Germany appeared in 1971 in the shape of a Setra S130 integral for Kirby's Coaches of Rayleigh in Essex. Owner Eddie Kirby had been impressed by Setras which he had seen while doing continental tours and approached Kassbohrer, the manufacturers of the Setra range. The company had tooled up to produce right-hand-drive models for sale in Africa, and added a coach for Kirby's to an African order. It was Mercedes-powered and remained unique in the UK. It would be the end of the 1970s before Setra started selling coaches in Britain, by which time the S130 had been superseded by the 200-series range.

Moseley's initial success with Caetano saw them make contact with another European-built body, with the announcement at the beginning of 1969 that the company was now an agent for Van Hool. A right-hand drive Van Hool-bodied Bedford VAL was shown at the Brussels show, complete with Moseley Continental lettering. To

Right above **The realisation that coaches could in some circumstances qualify for the government's new bus grant led to a rush of grant-specification vehicles. The Duple Viceroy Express had a wider entrance with jack-knife doors and a revised front dome which was deep enough to accommodate a good-sized destination display. The open door reveals the layout of the steps on the Ford R-series, which are turned towards the rear to avoid the engine. MacColl of Benderloch ran this R1014, bought new in 1972.** *Iain MacGregor*

Right below **Willowbrook at the start of the 1970s demonstrated its new-found independence from Duple by building a purpose-designed bus-grant coach, the Expressway. It sold in reasonable numbers to independents for a few years, mainly on Bedford and Ford chassis. Bowman of Craignure on the Isle of Mull bought one on a Ford R1114.** *Stewart J Brown*

suit UK tastes it had four main side windows instead of the standard seven of most Van Hool bodies of the time.

In the event, Van Hool sales in the UK were handled by Arlington which initially offered bodywork on the Bedford VAL and VAM, and soon added AEC and Leyland chassis too – a Van Hool-bodied Reliance operated by Best of Ealing won the Blackpool and Brighton coach rallies in 1972. Van Hool bodies were available on the Ford R226 (but not on the shorter R192) from 1971 through Don Everall, the Midlands-based Ford dealer.

Seddon had sold small numbers of coaches in the 1950s, and re-entered the market in the autumn of 1969, following some limited success in selling buses. The first new-generation coaches from the Oldham manufacturer were four front-engined Pennine IVs with Plaxton Panorama Elite bodies for Hanworth Acorn of Bedfont in Middlesex. The Pennine IV had a Perkins 6.354 5.8-litre engine rated at 120bhp and driving through an ENV five-speed manual gearbox. A Perkins V8 with 170bhp was available as an option. Its chassis price was £1,940, which made it a shade cheaper than a Bedford VAL, then costing just over £2,000. A Hanworth Acorn Seddon was entered in the 1970 Brighton coach rally, along with two others from Bicknell of Godalming and Wimbledon & Mitcham Belle Coaches.

At the 1970 Commercial Motor Show there were two Plaxton-bodied Pennine IVs in the demonstration park in the colours of Bullock of Cheadle and Knightswood of Watford. The latter clearly had a penchant for the unusual, having figured earlier in this story with an MCW-bodied Bedford. The SELNEC PTE, supporting local industry, also bought Seddon coaches.

Plaxton's successful Elite was given a new grille for the 1971 season, and this was unveiled at the 1970 Show as the Elite II. At this time there were changes afoot at Duple. The White

family which had set the business up, sold out to Frank B Ford. Ford had considerable experience in the coach industry, including a spell on the board of Plaxton. His arrival at Blackpool would set far-reaching changes in train.

The Bedford Y-series quickly proved as popular with independents as had most models before it. It also won Bedford added coach business from SBG, with Eastern Scottish taking Bedford YRQs with spacious 38-seat Alexander Y-type bodies for its tour fleet from 1971. These featured a revised grille which offered a greater air flow and was used on Y-types for all chassis makes irrespective of radiator or engine position – Bedford, Ford, AEC and Leyland. Other SBG companies buying lightweights – most notably Alexander (Northern) – were running R-series Fords.

SBG companies were still buying Alexander Y-types, but were increasingly treating them as dual-purpose vehicles and turning to Duple for real coaches. The only independent buying Y-types in the early 1970s was Premier Travel, and the creation of NBC saw Alexander being edged out of the new group's body orders. Few Alexander-bodied coaches were bought by NBC.

In 1968 the government had announced the introduction of a capital grant towards the purchase of new buses. This was designed to speed fleet modernisation, with an eye on hastening the introduction of one-man-operation which would help contain operators' rising costs. The grant was initially 25 per cent of the total cost of the vehicle, but from 1971 was raised to 50 per cent. At first sight this did not appear to have much to do with coaches, but it wasn't long before shrewd operators realised that here was a way of getting new coaches at a discount.

GBU 196K

Seddon tried to win a share of the market for bus-grant coaches with its Interurban body, mounted on a front-engined Pennine VI chassis. It was not a success. *Iain MacGregor*

More than ever it pays to—
CATCH A COACH

and enjoy built-in Bonuses – **1** Motorway Speed **2** Happy Family Travel **3** More Spending Money **4** Guaranteed Seat

Through and connecting services from all parts. Ask your Travel Agent or Local Bus Company

Provided the vehicle spent most of its time wholly or mainly on stage carriage services – the legal term at that time for a local bus service – it would be eligible for grant. This meant that coach operators who ran bus services could buy a new coach which met the bus grant specifications, collect the appropriate grant, and have the vehicle available for genuine coach work at weekends. At least 50 per cent of its mileage had to be on stage carriage services – a remarkably generous allowance which almost invited abuse of the grant – and this applied for the first five years of the vehicle's life, although the coach could be sold after two years and a proportion of the grant repaid.

The bus grant specifications set out minimum entrance widths, and to meet these both Duple and Plaxton produced bodies which were suitably modified and fitted with two-piece power-operated doors. Thus was born the Viceroy Express and the Elite Express, both with what were described as bus-grant doors and, on the Viceroy Express, a bigger roof-mounted destination display. The Elite Express was often fitted with what was known in the trade as a Bristol dome, a roof-mounted destination box which was a feature of most coach bodies fitted to Bristol chassis because the front-mounted radiator of the RE and LH precluded fitting any form of destination equipment below the windscreen. A small number of Caetano bodies were built to bus grant specifications. The first bus grant coaches were delivered by Plaxton in the summer of 1970.

Willowbrook had been sold by Duple in 1971 and it rose to the challenge of the bus grant coach in 1972 by introducing the Expressway, which had a two-piece door as standard and

large flat-glass side windows. Most Expressways (the design was also known as the 002) were dual-purpose vehicles and they were generally fitted to Bedford and Ford chassis, although small numbers were fitted to AEC, Leyland and Seddon chassis. Two Welsh operators – Llynfi of Maesteg and Silcox of Pembroke Dock – ordered Expressway bodies on Bristol LH chassis, but these were never built. One high-specification Expressway for The King's Ferry in Kent raised a few eyebrows when it won the 1974 Brighton coach rally. In all Willowbrook built around 150 of its Expressway model, most of which went to small fleets. The only big batches were for the Tyne & Wear PTE, with 10 Leyland Leopards, and South Wales Transport with 13 Bedfords.

Seddon was having some modest success in the supply of bus bodies and in 1972 produced an Interurban coach which with its shallow windows and flat-glass windscreens lacked the flair of Willowbrook's dual-purpose body. A demonstrator on a front-engined Pennine VI chassis made it to the demonstration park of the 1972 Earls Court Commercial Motor Show and was subsequently exported to Australia. Only one other Interurban coach was sold, on a Pennine VI to Princess Bus Service of Newcastle-under-Lyme.

The one operator which really took advantage of new bus grant to buy coaches was Barton Transport. In the 1960s Barton's fleet had been made up of an amazing assortment of new, used and rebuilt vehicles – the latter including 10 Barton BTS2s in 1969 which were rebuilds of 1950s AEC Reliance chassis, fitted

with new Plaxton coach bodies. But the company seized the opportunity to update its vehicles and, in one of the most remarkable turn-arounds ever seen in a British bus operator, set about replacing its entire fleet with new bus-grant coaches. In 1973 Barton ordered no fewer than 145 bus-grant coaches – a remarkable order by any standards. These were 73 Plaxton-bodied Leopards and 72 Duple-bodied Bedfords. By 1975 the entire 300-strong fleet would be made up of post-1970 coaches, with even the 1969 BTS2 rebuilds having been sold.

One of the problems of coach manufacture was the need to co-ordinate the production of chassis and bodies. This was amply illustrated when *Coaching Journal* visited Duple in 1970, at a time when chassis were in short supply and almost 300 completed bodies were standing on frames known as horses, waiting for the arrival of chassis.

Changing times

The Dominant by **DUPLE**

BRITAIN'S FINEST LUXURY COACH

In 1972 change was in the air. NBC announced a new corporate identity, including nationwide branding of its express coach operations under the National Travel banner and in an all-white livery. The familiar and colourful collection of company liveries would disappear. This had been hinted at as long ago as the start of 1970, when Tom Glass of NBC's Central Activities Group addressed the Chartered Institute of Transport: "There is a lot to be said for an over-all fleet name covering the coaches on the national network, and therefore we may see a single fleet name and an NBC symbol on these long-distance services."

It was the year when Duple launched a new all-metal body, the Dominant, the strongest body yet built by the company and one which followed Plaxton's lead by using gently curved side windows. Following the closure of Hendon and the sale of Willowbrook, all of Duple's coachbuilding activities were now concentrated in Blackpool. The Dominant replaced the Viceroy and was launched at the 1972 Show. However a strike at the Duple factory meant only one vehicle was on display to promote what was arguably the company's most significant new model since World War II.

The Dominant's shape, with gentle curvature to the sides, bore more than a passing similarity to Plaxton's Panorama Elite. And the reason for this was quite simple – Duple's design team was headed up by a recently-recruited ex-Plaxton engineer and a second-hand Elite was purchased from a London operator (by a Duple sales manager purporting to be buying it for a friend) and was taken apart at Blackpool.

The Dominant marked a change of emphasis for Duple and while it would undergo facelifts and restyling, it was a fully-engineered jig-built body planned for a long production life – in marked contrast to most of the models of the previous decades. A fully-laden prototype underwent 1,000 miles of testing on the cobbled pavé track at the Motor Industry Research Association, considered to be equal to 100,000 miles of normal operation.

The Dominant had interchangeable front and rear screens. And, echoing Plaxton's policy with the Elite, it ended the distinction between bodies built for light-weight and heavyweight chassis. The

Left top **Duple's new Dominant of 1972 copied the curved side windows which had been one of the talking points of the Plaxton Panorama Elite when it had been launched four years earlier. The SELNEC PTE was an early customer for the steel-framed Dominant and took five on Leyland Leopard chassis in 1973. It may claim to be on a continental tour – but it is actually in Greenock.**
Stewart J Brown

Dominant was a body for all full-size chassis. As always, progress had a price – in this case a whacking £1,000. In 1971 a Viceroy 37 body on a Ford R226 cost £5,520. In 1972 a Dominant on the replacement R1114 chassis cost £6,600 – a rise in price of almost 20 per cent. These were inflationary times. Britain had just decimalised, and some observers saw that as contributing to inflation as people were slow to realise that 2p was worth more than twice as much as 2d.

Duple's new all-steel body was received with widespread acclaim, although within a few years some of this would turn to criticism. Inadequate protection for the steel frame meant that early Dominants were plagued with corrosion problems. Plaxton would switch to an all-steel structure in 1974 when it introduced the Supreme.

As Duple launched the Dominant, Plaxton updated its Elite with new side mouldings and revised tail lights. In this, its final form, it was the Elite III. At the same time the Panorama body on the Bedford SB was given a new, more upright front end, with a strong resemblance to that on the Elite. Unusual Elites in the early 1970s were five on AEC Reliance chassis for Frames, which were of two-door layout. The second door was just ahead of the rear axle and was intended to speed the loading and unloading of tourists on London sightseeing tours. Frames had in 1967 taken over the Rickards business and some of the two-door Reliances carried Rickards livery. Another London operator, Glenton Tours, was specifying centre entrances on its Plaxton Elites at this time.

Leyland's Panther had not done well as a coach. The last two were built in 1972. They had Plaxton bodies and were for Skills of Nottingham, joining two bought in 1969. Only 24 PSUR1/2s were built and bodied as coaches for British fleets. Aside from any suspicion coach operators may have felt about rear engines – and having been faced with the Roadliner, Viking and Panther as the main contenders for their business, who could blame them for being suspicious? – the Panther also suffered from being more expensive than the proven and popular Leopard. In 1969 the list price of the Panther coach chassis was £3,815, compared with £3,270 for the PSU3/3R Leopard with manual gearbox or £3,475 for the PSU3A/4R Leopard with Pneumocyclic gearbox which was a more directly comparable specification.

Left middle **The rear-engined Leyland Panther found few buyers among coach operators. The last deliveries, to Skills of Nottingham in 1972, had Plaxton Panorama Elite bodies. Note the rare Panther badge.** *Stewart J Brown*

Left bottom **Most Alexander coach bodies in the 1960s and 1970s were based on the Y-type, but a few W-type buses found a role as express coaches, most notably with the Tyneside PTE and London Country Bus Services. The LCBS vehicles were 21 AEC Swifts for Green Line operation and entered service in 1972. They had originally been ordered by South Wales Transport but were diverted to LCBS as NBC tried to speed fleet replacement.** *Stewart J Brown*

Below **Park of Hamilton was an early customer for the Volvo B58. Seen soon after delivery in 1974, this one had a Duple Dominant body. By the end of 1974 Park would be Britain's biggest Volvo operator – with 11 B58s.** *Iain MacGregor*

AEC's companion to the Panther, the Swift, had not been promoted as a coach, but one batch of 21 was delivered to London Country Bus Services in 1972 with coach-seated Alexander W-type bodies. They were diverted from a South Wales Transport order and were allocated to the Green Line service running between Dartford and Heathrow Airport by way of Croydon. Other unusual coaches for Green Line operation were 90 AEC Reliance 691s with Park Royal 45-seat bodies. These had high-backed seats, and were thus more coach-like than the RMC and RCL class Routemasters which they were replacing. But the bodies were of bus rather than coach design, with double jack-knife doors, and a windscreen and front dash panel shared with contemporary Atlantean double-deckers for London Country. Even less coach-like were batches of bus-seated Leyland Nationals which carried NBC's local coach livery and which started to appear on Green Line services from the spring of 1973. Coach-seated Nationals would appear in 1974, but it would be 1977 before vehicles which most people would recognise as coaches appeared on Green Line routes.

London Country was not the only bus operator to run dual-purpose Alexander W-types. The Tyneside PTE had five on Leyland Panther bus chassis, bought for use on limited stop services in Newcastle.

Prior to 1972 virtually every new coach chassis in Britain was British built. The same had been true of trucks until the mid-1960s and it was the Volvo importer, Ailsa Trucks, which saw an opportunity in the coach market. An Ailsa Bus operation had been formed in 1971 to work on the Ailsa double-deck bus, and it took responsibility for the import and sales of the mid-engined B58 coach chassis from Sweden. The first was bodied as a demonstrator by Alexander using the ubiquitous Y-type, which perhaps made it something of a wolf in sheep's clothing. The B58 offered considerably more power – 230bhp from Volvo's 9.6-litre THD100 engine – than the existing sub-200bhp heavy-weight models, the Reliance and Leopard. It used a Volvo K19 five-speed gearbox which had synchromesh on the top four gears.

The second B58 to be bodied went to Plaxton, and appeared at the 1972 Commercial Motor Show. It was for Heyfordian of Upper Heyford. Yeates were appointed Volvo coach

dealers and the B58 got off to a flying start with over 40 in operation by the end of 1973, all bar the original demonstrator with Duple and Plaxton bodies, and mostly being delivered in ones and twos to small operators. The biggest user at this stage was Park of Hamilton with five.

Plaxton had expanded rapidly in the decade up to 1973. For the 1962-63 coaching season it had built fewer than 400 new coaches, the majority – 60 per cent – on Bedford chassis. Ten years later, for the 1972-73 season, output of coaches had risen to not far short of 1,400, with almost half of these being Bedfords, putting Plaxton well ahead of rivals Duple. Plaxton's growth had been helped by the Panorama Elite, which gave the Scarborough company the styling lead over Duple's Viceroy. It had also benefited from the closure of Harrington, and was winning business from NBC companies at a time when ECW was more interested in fulfilling large orders for buses. New bus grant also had an impact, as it fuelled demand for new coaches from operators large and small – the 1972-73 Plaxton build programme included 73 bus-grant coach bodies for Barton.

Two unusual coaches built by Plaxton in

1970 featured modified Derwent bus body shells with longer than normal fixed windows and forced-air ventilation for Neath & Cardiff Luxury Coaches. These were based on AEC Reliance chassis and were very similar in appearance to the standard 11m BET body shell of the period.

Despite Plaxton's impressive growth, imported bodywork was making gradual inroads. Caetano-bodied coaches were now a fairly common sight, generally with independents, although Doncaster Corporation bought two Estoril bodies on Ford R1114 chassis in 1973, marking the first appearance of Caetano in a public sector fleet. There were a few Van Hools around too, all with independents. Early 1970s Van Hool buyers included Limebourne of London, Best of Ealing, Court Line of Luton, Rennie of Dunfermline and Armchair of Brentford.

Another new name appeared at the 1972 Brighton rally with the odd combination of a Seddon chassis and Belgian-built Jonckheere bodywork for Musselwhite Coaches of Mosbrough, Derbyshire. Coach dealers Kirkby brought in a Jonckheere body on an AEC Reliance chassis and exhibited it at the 1972

Left **Subtle restyling saw the square look of the Caetano body being softened with some curvature being added to the lower front panels and a forward sloping pillar above the front wheelarch. Doncaster Transport was the first public sector operator to buy an imported coach body, taking two Caetano Estoril II bodies – as the restyled version was known – on Ford R1114 chassis in 1973.** *Michael Fowler*

Below left **In 1972 Jonckeere showed some interest in the UK market and a couple of bodies were imported. This one, a Solare on an AEC Reliance, was imported by coach dealers Kirkby and sold to The Kings ... ... In 1975 it was sold to Harris of Bro... ...was a 57-seater.** *Geoff Mills*

Below **Portuguese builder UTIC, which used AEC running units, sold a few Tagus coaches to British operators in the early 1970s. Ambassador Coaches of Edinburgh was one buyer. The Tagus used a rear-mounted AEC AH691 engine, as fitted to the AEC Reliance.** *Stewart J Brown*

Commercial Motor Show. But it would be the late 1970s before Jonckheere bodies became common.

Another Portuguese manufacturer to appear in Britain was UTIC, with the Tagus integral based on AEC running units. These, too, were imported by Moseley and the first two – for Supreme Coaches of Coventry – entered service in the autumn of 1972. The Tagus had a rear-mounted AEC AH691 engine and a ZF six-speed synchromesh gearbox. The styling was angular, with flat glass side windows and a comparatively shallow two-piece windscreen. An unusual feature was a retractable step below the entrance, which slid out when the two-piece glider doors were opened. The first imports to Britain had trouble with the doors beginning to open at 70mph, a problem solved by simply changing the air pressure of the door control system.

The steel-framed Tagus wasn't cheap, selling for £12,500. Nor, by the standards of the day, was it light, with an unladen weight of just under 9 tons, although it could still return fuel figures in the region of 12mpg. Sales were only just in double figures.

Bedford's unusual VAL came to the end of the road in 1972. In the 10 years since its launch over 1,900 had been supplied to UK coach operators, with the last few L-registered examples entering service during 1973. The vertical mid-engined YRQ had been a success, and the unorthodox VAL's replacement was a long-wheelbase version of the YRQ, the YRT, designed for 11m-long bodywork. The wheelbase was increased from 16ft 1in to 18ft 6in.

AEC upgraded its Reliance coach chassis in 1973 by fitting as standard the 12.4-litre AH760 engine in place of the 11.3-litre AH691. Power was increased from 154bhp to 165bhp.

East Kent's first 36ft-long coaches had been 20 AEC Reliances with Park Royal bodies in 1962. As these reached their tenth anniversary the company took the decision to extend their lives by scrapping the rather bus-like Park Royal bodies and having new Plaxton Panorama Elite II bodywork fitted. This took place in 1972-73. Ten similar 1963 coaches received new Plaxton bodies in 1974. After rebodying they served East Kent for a further 10 years.

NBC subsidiaries were busily applying white paint to their existing coaches, which included some rather bizarre vehicles such as centre-

entrance Duple Britannias acquired from Samuelson by the London-based National Travel operation. White paint was also being applied to coaches running on National Travel's express services, resulting in all-white BMMO CM6Ts carrying somewhat inappropriate Midland Red fleetnames. But National Travel was also looking at alternatives for the future and in 1972-73 took two odd coaches into stock.

The least odd was an Alexander M-type, a model which was successfully running between Scotland and London. The Scottish Bus Group's M-types were on Bristol RE chassis (other types would follow later in the decade), but National Travel's was on a 12m PSU5 Leopard. It was an exhibit at the 1972 Commercial Motor Show and was allocated initially to Ribble. It was the only M-type built for service by an operator outside SBG.

Rather more unusual was a Scania CR145, which was completed at Birmingham by MCW (at that time involved with Scania on the Metro-Scania urban bus). The CR145 was a rear-engined integral, powered by a 260bhp 14.2-litre Scania D14 engine. It had 37 seats and a toilet and was part of National Travel's

drive to find a vehicle suitable for sustained high-speed cruising on the motorway network, spending some time on loan from MCW. Its white livery and uncompromisingly square lines in the era of gently curved Duples and Plaxtons earned it the unflattering sobriquet of the Flying Shoe Box.

NBC also looked at the eight-wheeled Moulton prototype in 1972, but didn't actually run it. This was a futuristic-looking 11.3m-long integral with running units from British Leyland's light truck range and a front-mounted Perkins engine. Moulton was looking for someone to build it (Leyland and Dennis both examined the design but turned it down) but this unusual coach was to get no further than being a prototype. The use of eight wheels and Hydragas suspension (another Moulton development which was used in BMC cars) promised a high-quality ride.

When National Travel was launched, it was running in a world which had changed since the start of the motorway era almost 15 years before. The number of cars had effectively doubled, from 6 million to 12 million in round figures. The effect of this rise in car ownership on

Below **The new National Travel identity was applied to coaches operated by NBC companies from 1972. Among the more unusual vehicles to be repainted white was this 1961 AEC Reliance operated by Samuelsons. It has a centre-entrance Duple Britannia body.** *Stewart J Brown*

Bottom **National Travel's search for a coach which offered improved standards of comfort and performance led to it testing a Scania CR145 in 1973. Scania was at that time working closely with MCW and the coach was promoted as the MCW 145 – but none were sold.** *Stewart J Brown*

bus services is widely recognised, but it hit coach travel too. The day tour market vanished in many places, as excursionists used the flexibility provided by their cars to plan their own itineraries and timetables. Express coaching and the private hire market were hit as well. It would take coach deregulation in 1980 to revitalise express services and see fares drop and service frequencies rise.

The decline in coach travel saw the end of one of the oldest names in the business – Birch Bros. The Birch history could be traced back to the middle of the 19th century, but it came to an end in 1971 when what remained of the company – nine coaches – was acquired by the Ewer Group, owners of Grey-Green and its associates. The Birch name lived on until 1977, which was one of the conditions of the sale. Birch had earlier pulled out of express service operation, selling its London to Rushden service and the 12 Leyland Leopard coaches which operated it to United Counties in 1969.

Another old-established coach company to cease at this time was Hall Bros of South Shields, whose operations included a daily express service to Coventry. Hall Bros had a 35-strong fleet of modern coaches and was bought by Barton Transport in 1967, being absorbed into the Barton business in 1971.

In Scotland, David MacBrayne whose coaches and steamers were synonymous with the Scottish Highlands, was brought under the control of the Scottish Transport Group. This saw MacBrayne's holiday coach tour operations being taken over by Alexander (Midland), while its coach services were shared between Highland Omnibuses and Western SMT.

Two of the four PTEs set up under the 1968 Transport Act developed coach operations. SEL-NEC Travel was running Bedford VALs and VASs, alongside Seddon Pennines and Leyland Leopards. The Tyneside PTE bought two old-established coach business in the summer of 1973 – Armstrong of Westerhope and the associated Galley's Coaches company. Between them they operated 30 vehicles, most of which were Plaxton-bodied Bedfords. Tyneside had briefly tried running coaches in 1971 when it bought three Bedford YRQs with Duple Viceroy bodies, but these had been withdrawn at the end of 1972. From 1974 it would start buying new heavyweight coaches to replace the Bedfords acquired from Armstrong and Galley's.

Below **From 1972 NBC subsidiaries' coaches and dual-purpose vehicles which were not intended for front-line service received what was known as local coach livery under the group's corporate identity programme. This used red or green for the lower half of the body with white for the top. An unusual coach in the Hants & Dorset fleet shows the effect. It is a former Southdown Leyland Leopard with the big-windowed version of Weymann's Castilian body, a body style supplied only to Southdown.** *Chris Aston*

Bottom **The short 10m-long Leyland Leopard PSU4 was a relatively rare choice for a coach, being little cheaper than the more common 11m-long PSU3. Most PSU4 coaches went to BET or ex-BET companies. In 1970 Trent took five, with roomy 40-seat Plaxton Panorama Elite bodywork, one of which is seen in Llandudno in 1973 after being repainted in National white – a livery which would become recognised country-wide as the decade progressed.** *Iain MacGregor*

Rationalisation by NBC saw some old names vanish. Charlie's Cars was absorbed by the associated Shamrock & Rambler company in 1970 – both were Bournemouth-based independents which had been bought by THC in 1966. South Midland, which had been operated as part of Thames Valley, was put under the control of City of Oxford Motor Services. In Wales, the operations of Neath & Cardiff Luxury Coaches were taken over by South Wales Transport. Both were former BET companies.

But the big changes would come at the end of 1973, with the creation of regional National Travel companies. National Travel (North East) took over Hebble (by then the coaching arm of Yorkshire Woollen) and Sheffield United. The operations of North Western Road Car and Standerwick passed to National Travel (North West). National Travel (South East) took over the businesses run by Tillings Travel, Timpson and Samuelson. The last of the original National Travel companies, South West, took over the operations of Black & White and Greenslades'. The latter had already absorbed the Grey Cars operations of Devon General. Other names which were victims of the new regime were Royal Blue and Bristol Greyhound.

Coaches which were not intended for front-line operation received local coach livery in which the lower half of the coach was painted poppy red or leaf green, and the upper half white. This layout had been selected after considering the reverse, with a white lower half and coloured upper section, which had been applied experimentally to a Midland Red Willowbrook-bodied Leopard. Vehicles to receive local coach livery included types such as Bristol REs with bus-shell ECW dual-purpose bodies (although some were painted all-over white); London Country's Green Line coach-seated Leyland Nationals; and a batch of unusual Northern Counties-bodied Leopard express coaches delivered to Southdown in 1969

Setting sentiment to one side, it does seem strange to abandon respected names with a loyal local following. But – with the American Greyhound operation as the inspiration – that's what happened. And it's a fitting point at which to stop. In many ways coaching was in the doldrums. But not for long. The 1980 Transport Act and the deregulation which it brought, would inject new ideas into the coach industry. But that, as they say, is another story.

What's in a name?

Cosy Coaches, Happy Days, Sunny Hours – these were some of the more whimsical names used by 1960s coach operators. The vast majority of companies were family run businesses trading under the family name. The 1962 edition of *Passenger Transport Yearbook* lists, for example, no fewer than 67 Smiths – the best known being two in Lancashire, Smith's Tours (Wigan) and Ellen Smith of Rochdale. It also has 18 Browns. But many companies chose rather more descriptive names.

Colour was an obvious choice. Blue featured in the names of 28, with Blue Belle and Blue Bird being popular. Red features in 14. Next came silver in nine, including three Silver Queens, two Silver Stars and two Silverlines. Seven used cream, while five used green (not counting London Transport's Green Line). Other less popular colours were gold, grey, orange and yellow. And there were three Black & White companies – one being the famous Cheltenham operator. London's Green Line

theme was, incidentally, echoed in Gold Line (Dunoon), Red Line (of which there were three, in Kent, London and on Jersey), Blue Line (at Hedon, East Yorkshire), the two Silverlines (in Newport and Keighley) and Grayline in Bicester.

Other popular names included Enterprise (of which there were 11), Central (eight), Victoria (seven), variations on a Primrose theme (seven), Premier (seven) followed by Empress, Imperial, Progress and Pioneer. Only one coach operator claimed to be Popular (in Canning Town of all places), but five were Happy – Happy Days (Stafford) , Happy Times (Wednesfield) and on the Isle of Man where three happy operators vied for business: Happy-go-lucky, Happy Wanderers and Happy Ways. Two Midlands operators traded as De Luxe, and there were four using the rather homely Cosy Coaches title.

Animals featured too. There were three felines, Black Cat, Lion Services and Tiger Coaches, no doubt keeping out of the way of the

two Greyhounds and the solitary Whippet. There were also two Seagull Coaches – in the coastal resorts of Great Yarmouth and Blackpool – two Swallows, which presumably made a summer, one Bluebird and one Golden Eagle (as well as two ordinary Eagles). The weather featured in three Sunbeams, one Sunniways and Sunny Hours.

Happy Days indeed.

One of the best-known names based on colours was Grey-Green of London. Many Grey-Green coaches incorporated prominent destination displays, as shown on this Harrington Cavalier on the company's East Anglian express service. New in 1963, it is on a Leopard L2 chassis. *Paul Caudell*

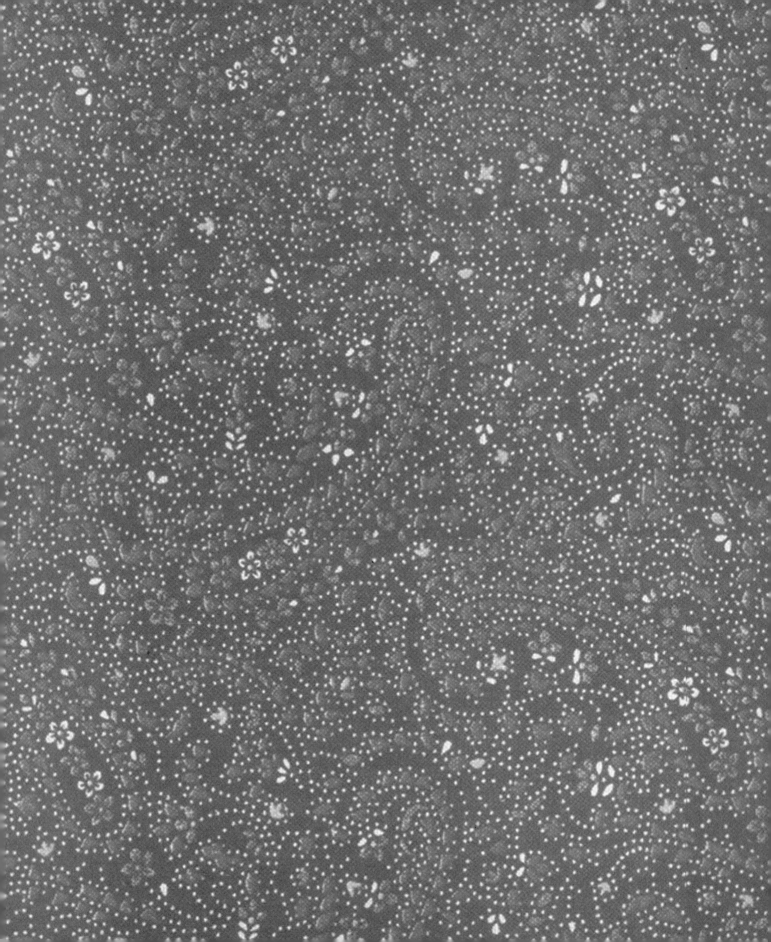